THE EXCHANGE STUDENT
SURVIVAL KIT

THE EXCHANGE STUDENT SURVIVAL KIT

Bettina Hansel

INTERCULTURAL PRESS, INC.

Yarmouth, Maine

For information, contact:
Intercultural Press, Inc.
P.O. Box 700
Yarmouth, Maine 04096, USA
207-846-5168

Book design and production by Patty J. Topel
Cover design by Letter Space

Printed in the United States of America.

02 01 00 99 98 97   4 5 6 7 8 9

Library of Congress Cataloging-in-Publication Data

Hansel, Bettina
   The exchange student survival kit/Bettina Hansel.
      p.   cm.
   Includes index.
   ISBN 1-877864-17-X
   1. Foreign study—United States. 2. Student exchange programs—United States. 3. Cultural relations. 4. High school
students—United States—Attitudes. I. Title.

LB1696.H36   1993
370.19'62—dc20   93-10449
                                                        CIP

For Jay and Clare

CONTENTS

Acknowledgments

An exchange organization such as AFS Intercultural Programs is based on the conviction that it is both desirable and possible to cross the cultural barriers that exist between us, wherever in the world we might live. In the more than twelve years I have spent with AFS, I have met people from all around the world who have reached out to me across these barriers. Many of them have become close and dear to me, even though large distances keep us separated. Some of them will recognize their own experiences in the examples presented. Still many others have passed through and left deep and lasting impressions, even though we somehow have lost contact with each other. Their stories are often used here, too.

In writing this, I would like to acknowledge all these people whose stories appear in these pages and to extend a special thanks to AFS Intercultural Programs, the organization that has brought most of these people into my life and made stories like these happen.

I would also like to extend my deepest appreciation for the research grant received from the Indo-American Fellowship program through which I again had the experience of being a foreigner and which introduced me to the experiences of numerous Indians who have studied in the United States. As well, I acknowledge with appreciation the graphs depicting the stages of the exchange student experience taken from *Host Family Survival Kit* by Nancy King and Ken Huff, published by the Intercultural Press. Finally, I would like to thank the Intercultural Press for recognizing the need for this handbook, and for the encouragement and support of David Hoopes and Toby Frank.

Bettina Hansel
New York City

January 19, 1993

Preface

When Bettina Hansel asked me to write the preface for *The Exchange Student Survival Kit*, I immediately accepted. Now having read the guide, I am even more pleased to write this preface because her book has real merit.

My phone rang early in 1963. I had been selected to take part in the first year-long program in South Africa sponsored by the American Field Service (AFS). I was going to be living with an English-speaking family in what was then the outskirts of Johannesburg and attending an English-style boarding school as a day student. I couldn't have been more surprised. I had applied for a Southern Hemisphere program because I had been studying Spanish, and the vast majority of countries listed were in South and Central America. I was certain they'd place me in a Spanish-speaking country. Wrong! It was the first of a number of surprises in a year-long adventure that shaped my life. It included tagging along with a woman doctor in the townships of Soweto and being on a train that was hit by a herd of elephants as we chugged through the Wankie Game Reserve—not to mention sleeping in a treehouse in the reserves, staring at the bejeweled eyes of tigers and leopards in the African night. Looking back now after eighteen years as a correspondent for ABC news, I realize my first journalistic experience came as a "foreign correspondent" writing articles from South Africa for my high school newspaper.

If you're looking at this book, you want to become an exchange student or you're at least thinking about it. It's an exciting adventure. Bettina Hansel writes straight from the heart. This survival kit gives you good, solid advice about culture shock, how to adjust to a host family, and where to park your cultural baggage while living abroad. She gives a host of examples to illustrate what she means. She knows what she is talking about. She has worked for and with exchange students for twelve years at American Field Service. How I wish I'd had this survival kit before I set out. It would have made it so much easier.

It's a challenge to live in a foreign country, speak a foreign language, and get used to strange customs. Nevertheless, being an exchange student will change your life and your thinking. It will make you a better person and, for those of you who have doubts, it is worth the effort. If you're like me you'll end up with two families for life: your own plus the one you live with as an exchange student.

So sit down, relax, and dig into this "How to" manual. This survival kit is a good road map for one of the greatest adventures you'll ever have. Good Luck!

Bettina Gregory
Washington, D.C.
October 1992

Introduction

Every year thousands of secondary school students leave their homes and families to travel hundreds, or thousands, of miles to unfamiliar countries, to live for a year with a family of total strangers, and to go to school where lessons are taught in a language different from the one they speak and understand. Why are there so many young people just like you who become exchange students every year? And why are there hundreds of programs offering this sort of experience to young people all over the world? Since you are an exchange student yourself (or thinking about becoming one), maybe you have some answers to these questions. Perhaps you've had to answer questions of friends or relatives who do not understand why you want to do this. Maybe you're beginning to wonder yourself why you decided to be an exchange student.

Students have been traveling abroad to study for centuries, but the high school exchange student is a relatively new traveler. Most of the major exchange programs for secondary school students came into existence following the Second World War. Their sponsors sought to promote understanding between peoples, to heal the wounds of the war. If an American family could host a young German or Japanese student, or if American, English, or French students could live for a while with a German family, then maybe feelings of friendship would grow in place of hatred and mistrust—certainly a daring goal for a troubled time.

Today, of course, we still live in troubled times, and healing is needed as much as ever. In the decades since World War II, the world has seen many conflicts, major and minor, between nations. Scars from long and difficult wars such as Vietnam and the shifting but constant crisis in the Middle East have marked entire generations in those areas and countries. Even the memories of the Second World War still linger like ghosts and leave a painful reminder of the need for tolerance and understanding among peoples. After forty years, a young German girl and her American

Jewish host family had to struggle with this history. "I had never thought much about Jewish people or World War II," she said. "My parents were children then, and my grandfather never discussed it. But to my host family, the war experience was still very real and immediate. We talked about it a lot. It was good for both of us." For the host mother, these discussions led to "a great, wonderful healing" that was a very special part of the family's experience with the German girl.

Today's world is rapidly changing. New conflicts continue to erupt between nations. While we live in the wake of a world that was for years controlled by opposing superpowers, the ending of the Cold War has not brought the hoped-for peace. Our world remains divided for myriad reasons. Modern communications and transportation have greatly increased contact between cultures but have not increased their understanding of each other. In fact, there may be more opportunity for misunderstanding than ever before. More communication is taking place between people of different cultures who give very different meanings to the messages that are sent.

Exchange programs by themselves will never bring peace to the world, but they do provide a way for young people to live in another culture and learn how other people give meaning to their own lives and to the messages they send and receive. This is an important reason for being an exchange student. Although you see yourself—and others may see you—as an "ambassador" representing your country overseas, your primary goal will be to learn about your host country and culture and about yourself. Your year abroad is intended to be a very special educational experience.

What can you learn as an exchange student? You may think first about learning a foreign language. Since you'll need to use the language to communicate with your hosts, you will have plenty of motivation to learn it. Whether you've just started or whether you've studied it for years, your fluency is going to improve because you'll be using the new language in much the same way as you did when you learned your own language.

But communication and understanding involve more than just knowing the language. You may already understand the words perfectly in a language, but still miss the meaning of a spoken sentence. For example, you might not understand a joke someone tells you because you haven't experienced the situation that makes it funny. Or, you may be confused by some conversation between two people because you don't understand the roles that different people play in that culture.

During your year abroad, you will build the experience you need to make sense of the jokes and the role-defined relationships. Even if your exchange program is shorter, the impact of living in another culture is great.[1] You'll come to understand the significance of certain ways of saying things and of different behaviors. Events will have special meanings, and the right thing to say or do will depend on the situation. What you'll be learning is a different way of looking at the world, that is, the way it's seen by the culture of the people who live in the country you're going to visit.

But, you may ask, why is it so important to learn these things? What's so good about learning how to see the world from a different perspective from your own?

While you were growing up, you were taught certain ways to behave. You learned that some things were good and some were bad, some right, some wrong. You learned to like certain things (people, places, food, appearances, etc.) and dislike others. You learned the correct way to talk or communicate with others according to who they were (friend, parent, teacher) and to their rank, age, or other factors. You learned how you should behave and how you shouldn't, what you should believe and what you shouldn't. You even learned how to think and learn in the particular ways people in your society think and learn. There are two important things to understand about what you were taught and what you learned as you grew up: (1) that all these rights, wrongs, goods, bads, shoulds, and shouldn'ts are what define the culture you live in and carry inside you and (2) that every culture is different and teaches its children its own distinctive rights and wrongs. In short, different cultures have different ways of looking at and valuing life. They have different outlooks and perspectives that are embodied in their ways of thinking, behaving, and communicating. And this is what is so important about the opportunity to learn which the exchange experience offers. By being able to encounter and learn about how another culture sees and responds to life and the world, you gain a sharper image and better understanding of your own culture and your own outlook on life. You also develop the ability to adapt to other cultures by coming to understand that these kinds of differences are normal and okay. What you believe to be right or wrong and how you behave depends on what you have learned in your own particular culture.

New ideas from another culture will challenge your thinking and bring your attention to aspects of your life at home that you wouldn't ordinarily notice. Shu-Mei had never made decisions alone in China. She discussed her opinions openly with her parents and her friends, but it was never up to her to decide what to do. Much of the time, her parents or her teachers told her what she should do. Even when adults weren't involved, such as when her friends got together for games and parties, the activities were typically planned in advance, and Shu-Mei always went along with what the group was doing. But here in the United States, she was often expected to be independent in her decisions. "Decide for yourself," was the expected pattern. People expected her to make all sorts of major and minor decisions on her own. In her new school, she even had to choose what classes to take, but this made no sense to her. What did she know about what was appropriate to take? She had a counselor from the school to help, but this woman kept asking her, "What do *you* think you should take?" Shu-Mei had no idea. Later, after she was enrolled, the social studies teacher wanted her to state her own opinions on current issues. As far as Shu-Mei could see, she had no opinions to offer. But decisions were a constant part of school. On tests she had to decide which essay questions to answer. She had to decide which sport to play in gym class. Her host family expected her to make a lot of her own decisions, too. What kind of sandwich did she want to have for lunch? What did she want to drink? When did she want to do her homework? What did she want to wear to school? Shu-Mei found it difficult and often exhausting to have to make so many little decisions about everyday life. How could she know what would be best?

In thinking about her problem, Shu-Mei realized that it was important for Americans to be able to make all these decisions themselves. She began to watch the Americans around her and ask them questions about why they behaved the way they did. She noticed that even her little four-year-old host brother, Tommy, was encouraged to select his own clothes each day, and, even though the shirts and pants were often mismatched, Linda, his mother, almost always let him wear what he had picked. This surprised Shu-Mei, so she asked Linda about it. Linda explained how important she felt it was for Tommy to be able to manage on his own and make his own decisions without relying too much on his mother all the time. This was a very surprising idea for Shu-Mei and her first real introduction to the concepts of American individualism and independence. Tommy was being taught how to make decisions so that when he was older, it would be easy for him to make the kind of decisions that Shu-Mei was now finding so difficult.

Shu-Mei's learning was not just about the United States and its individualistic culture. She was also learning more about what it means to be Chinese and how this was an important part of her identity. In contrasting the Chinese patterns and values with those of the United States, Shu-Mei gained new insight into her own culture. Learning about one's own culture and values is an essential part of the exchange experience. You become more aware of the patterns your culture has set that guide your behavior and reactions. You try new ways of doing things, so you can also discover your hidden talents, learn new skills, and create fresh possibilities for your life.

This process we have just described is called *intercultural learning*. Intercultural learning does not happen to you simply by going abroad, however. It's likely to be one of your greatest educational challenges. Your new friends and family will have many surprising values and attitudes. They probably have strange ways of behaving, too. Some of these differences will seem new and exciting. Some things you'll like better than what you have in your own country.

Other differences will be difficult for you to accept. At times you may feel angry, insulted, confused, or embarrassed.

For Jaime, an exchange student from Colombia, the variety of courses offered in his U.S. high school was a big improvement in his mind from the situation in his Colombian school. He was thrilled that he could take photography and journalism as school courses. He imagined an exciting new career for himself, traveling around the world as a photojournalist. However, in his host family he experienced another difference that was not so pleasing to him. His host mother expected him to help with the "women's work" of washing the dishes and cleaning the house. He could only feel insulted at being asked to do these chores—which he would never have been asked to do at home—and he couldn't believe that anyone would treat him this way.

Similarly, Frances, an American girl visiting Sweden, could not believe how much freedom her host parents gave her. For the first time in her life she felt she was treated as an adult. Her host family trusted her completely and did not set curfews for her when she went out with her friends. But she was very uncomfortable with the family's disregard for religion. They did not seem to take her seriously when she tried to talk to them about her faith, and they had no interest in going to church with her. She often found herself in tears trying to convince the family that she was right.

With the help of warm and loving host families and concerned adults in the community, both of these students eventually learned to accept the differences they found, both those they liked and those they didn't. Jaime gradually understood that, in the United States, washing dishes was not solely women's work and he was able to do his chores without feeling any resentment or insult. Frances decided to accept her hosts as good, loving people whose beliefs were of an entirely different nature from her own. She did not reject her beliefs, but she became better able to tolerate other beliefs even when they contradicted her own.

Some differences will be challenging in another way. You'll find things in the host country that won't make sense to you or that seem stupid or crazy. With patience, you will usually be able to find an explanation that is neither stupid nor crazy. For example, one

American student who went to Japan reported:

> I couldn't understand why my Japanese family had
> an electric dish-drying machine. To me, it would
> make sense to have a dishwasher, but if you didn't
> have one, you could certainly leave the dishes to
> dry by themselves rather than use a machine. Later
> someone explained to me that drying dishes in the
> air wouldn't be sanitary. So I realized that the
> machine wasn't so much to save work as to dry the
> dishes in a sanitary way.

It may seem trivial to talk about such things as differences in the way dishes are dried, but it is often in these very ordinary activities that deep cultural attitudes are most firmly rooted—in this case, attitudes about cleanliness and about the uses of machinery. As an exchange student, you have the chance to experience everyday activities which will eventually lead to encounters with deep cultural differences. You will struggle with curious values and strange ideas, and you will have to make sense out of the confusion you feel.

It is often said that nothing of value is easily attained. This is certainly true of genuine understanding between people and of the learning that occurs in the intercultural experience. These are the challenges the exchange program offers you. This book is designed to help insure that you can meet them.

Being an exchange student is not easy, and not always fun, so you need a "survival kit" to keep you going at times. Explorers going into uncharted territory will take along a small bag or kit filled with a variety of items—medical supplies, matches, canned food, etc.—that may be useful or essential as they try to survive in the wilderness. This book, like a survival kit, holds a variety of ideas, hints, or suggestions that will help you succeed and navigate the uncharted, or at least unfamiliar, country to which you are headed. We suggest you not read it once and set it aside. Read it straight through—before you leave or after you arrive at your destination—but then return to it again after you've had some substantial experience in your host country. Each step of the way, you will find something that will be enlightening and valuable to you in your effort to have a successful exchange experience.

Your exchange year is likely to be a very intense, very emotional time. Your reward will be the relationships you build that can last a lifetime. The experience you have will continue to shape the way you live for years to come.

Note: For students visiting the United States, this book is designed to be a companion publication to *The Host Family Survival Kit: A Guide for American Host Families* by Nancy King and Ken Huff (Yarmouth, ME: Intercultural Press, 1985) in which the patterns of intercultural learning and cross-cultural adaptation are discussed from the perspective of the host family. It focuses on the same principal adjustment and communication issues and uses the same eight stages to examine the experience in detail. Students and host families may want to use the two books together as a basis for discussions designed to enrich the experience and/or solve problems in their relationship which may arise from time to time.

---

[1]A discussion of shorter exchange programs is found in the appendix.

Part I

On Being an Exchange Student

1

What Does It Mean to Be an Exchange Student?

Being an exchange student means having a special status. The selection process for exchange students often includes a series of tests or interviews, and students must be recommended by their teachers for most programs. Being selected as an exchange student singles you out among your peers. You were clearly among the best in some way, and now you're going to represent your country and community abroad. You probably feel your special status even before you leave your country, especially if your school or community decides to honor you in a formal way because you are taking part in the exchange program.

Even everyday conversations are filled with mention of your impending travel. Friends at school, neighbors, and others you meet in the weeks before your departure start to show a new sort of interest in you and ask, "When do you leave?" or tell you something of their own travels or others they have known from the county you'll be visiting. "Send me a postcard." "Take plenty of pictures." "Bring me back some blue jeans." Or even advice: "Don't drink the water." You might be given new luggage or other special gifts to take with you. Everything about what you do and who you are seems tied up in the fact of your being an exchange student.

In your host country, you continue to be an extraordinary person, treated specially perhaps, because you are an exchange student. But you are also extraordinary because you are completely outside of your normal environment. You have come to a new family, a new community, a new school. You find yourself among strangers. How do you fit in? Where is there something familiar for you?

YOUR ROLE IN THE FAMILY

The exchange organization has placed you in a host family for two reasons. First, because the family is the heart of the culture, and you will learn the most in this setting. Second, because the family can offer you support as you try to cope with the many changes you'll face during your year abroad.

What will your role in the host family be? The exchange student and host-family relationship is not one that has a long precedent in most cultures. Frequently students and their families begin their experience by trying to fit each other into roles that are familiar to them. Most often these roles are inappropriate. Here are some of the things that you are not:

You are not a houseguest. One familiar role is that of the house guest. You have no doubt been a houseguest at some time when visiting a friend or relative in another city. You probably stayed for only a few days or at most a few weeks. When you are a houseguest, the family you're visiting prepares special meals for you, takes you sightseeing, and otherwise tries to keep you entertained. They may use the best dishes while you're visiting. You may be given the best bed. You are not asked to help with the housework. Every effort is made to be sure you are comfortable and to make your short-term visit pleasant. The normal family routines are altered. Members of the family are likely to behave in a more formal way among themselves than when no guests are present.

While the rules of hospitality vary from culture to culture, in no culture should a host family and their exchange student maintain this sort of relationship for an entire year together. In the early days of your stay with them, you may discover that your host family treats you as they would a houseguest, but it is important to leave that role behind as soon as possible so that you both can feel more at home.

You are not a boarder. Exchange students sometimes take the attitude that the fees they pay for the exchange program include room and board with a family. Because they think of themselves as paying guests, they do little to participate in the life of the family. This attitude defeats the purpose of the exchange program, which is to provide the opportunity for intercultural learning, and can leave the host family, who generously volunteered to welcome the exchange student into their home, feeling like servants. In most cases, the families are not paid fees by the exchange organization. If they are, fees are often a contribution toward the cost of having you stay in their home. The sponsoring organization should be able to give you guidelines as to the appropriate behavior in that situation.

You are not a housekeeper or babysitter. While you will probably be asked to do your share of the household chores and may, from time to time, be asked to take care of any small children in the home, you should not be doing more work than is expected of the other members of the family. You have not come to do domestic work for your host family, but to learn and to share in their family life.

If you are not any of these things as an exchange student, what are you?

Are you a member of the family? In many ways you *are* like a member of the family. The host parents assume responsibility for your basic well-being. Like any parents, they make certain that you have enough to eat and have a comfortable room. They are concerned about your health and your adjustment to school. They are interested in you, and ultimately they will worry about you.

In other important ways you are not fully a member of the family. You have not shared their experiences and do not share their memories, even though they will likely tell you stories about things that have happened to them in the past and show you photos or films of some of these events. You may feel this difference sharply when the family members get together with other relatives.

More important, you have another, real family which is ultimately responsible for your well-being. The host parents are very much aware of their obligation to your parents. They may be more protective of you than of their own children for this reason. At the same time, they may give you special privileges or may hesitate to impose their rules on you because they know that your own parents have established different rules. As one host father commented:

> If she were really my own daughter, I'd know
> where my authority would lie. For example, when
> she refused to try on that coat we found for her—
> if that had been my own daughter, I would have
> said, "Put it on and wear it because it's perfectly
> good." But I wouldn't say that to her, because I'm
> not really her father.

The situation is similar for you, too. You cannot always behave
toward the host parents as you do toward your own parents. Perhaps
you are affectionate with your own parents, but feel peculiar
hugging or kissing your host parents. You may argue occasionally
with your own parents but feel that arguing with your hosts would
be rude and ungrateful.

And what should you call them? You cannot go through the
entire year tapping them on the shoulder or waiting to get their
attention before speaking to them simply because you do not know
what to call them. Many exchange students call their host parents
"Mom" and "Dad" because this is what the other children in the
family call them. Also, these terms are often different from the
words for "Mom" and "Dad" in their own language, which can be
reserved to refer to their parents back home. Other exchange
students prefer to use the first names of their host parents or select
an affectionate nickname to use. Some students simply ask their
hosts, "What would you like me to call you?" Whatever you decide,
you should settle this issue right at the start because having no name
to call your hosts is uncomfortable for everyone.

Most host families also have children of their own, and you may
wonder what relationship you will have with them. Your feelings
about your host siblings are not likely to be the same as your feelings
for your own brothers and sisters. They may not be prepared to
accept you right away in this role either. A young American girl
whose family hosted a Kenyan boy remarked, "As soon as he arrived
he said, 'I'm going to be your big brother now. I'm going to be your
parents' son.' I didn't like that at all." In another family, a young
host brother resented that his mother was uncritical of the ex-

change student's habit of leaving her wet towels lying around the house. When the mother reminded her son that he also left his towels where they didn't belong, he complained, "But I live here."

Because you are new to the family, because you're from a different country, and because you need to find out things, you will get extra attention from the parents and from the family's friends and relatives. When Aunt Sue used to visit her favorite niece, Karen, she always had a sympathetic ear for Karen's problems with boyfriends or with her parents. Now when Aunt Sue visits, Åsa, the exchange student from Norway, is always part of the conversation, and somehow the focus is now on Åsa and Norway and never on Karen. Karen likes Åsa and is not normally resentful, but she sometimes can't help wishing that Åsa would disappear for a while.

Of course, not all host siblings are upset by the attention or the position that the exchange student has in their family, but your arrival does change the dynamics in the family, especially among the children. Though the specific patterns vary from family to family, there are typically certain attitudes, responsibilities, or privileges associated with being the oldest or the youngest in the family. With your arrival, the oldest child in the family may now be you! Or simply because of the different experience you have had, you may be more mature in some areas than the brother or sister of the same age. Or perhaps you are neater with your belongings, or more interested in your studies, or you like to read more than the children in the family. Suddenly, you are the shining example for the other children, who may feel that their parents were perfectly content with their behavior until *you* came along.

You may introduce new ideas and routines that pose a challenge to the way the family lives. Amy's parents always made her go to bed by 10:30, but they let Chieko from Japan stay up as long as she wanted—often well past midnight. Issues like this can cause the children in the family to want or expect similar privileges and attention from their parents.

Exchange students sometimes feel great pressure to win the approval of the host parents, but it is often the relationship with the other teenagers in the house that can make the family experience either satisfying or uncomfortable. Of course, this doesn't mean that your relationship with the parents is unimportant. It does mean that you also need to form direct, personal relationships with the children in the family and be sensitive to their feelings and needs.

For the most part, your host brothers or sisters will be eager to spend time with you and introduce you to their friends, but you should also plan to find friends of your own in the community. Even though you may get along very well with the children in the family and like being with them, your host brothers or sisters are probably not going to be your best friends and it will be better if you are not totally dependent on them.

YOUR ROLE IN THE COMMUNITY

In some schools and communities, the exchange student is given special treatment. If you are in such a place, newspaper articles may be written to announce your arrival. A school assembly may be convened to introduce you to the other students. In other places, though, the exchange student is barely noticed. It is not possible to predict the reception you will have in your school or community, although in large, cosmopolitan cities it is less likely that you will receive any special notice since your presence is not so unusual.

Even if your arrival is hardly observed in any official way, you'll still be seen as a representative of your home country. You'll probably be asked many questions about your life at home, some of which may sound rather stupid to you, especially if the people in your host community tend not to be familiar with your country. A girl from the former Soviet republic of Georgia was asked if there were any trees in her country, and many of the Americans she met confused her country with the state of Georgia in the United States. You may also hear criticism of your government and somehow be made to feel directly responsible for whatever sorts of problems there may be back home. Holly from Wisconsin frequently heard bitter complaints about U.S. foreign policy when she was in Argentina. She knew little about the situations and policies that were being criticized, and yet she was made to feel as if it were her fault, or at least something she should correct. In these situations, it is normal to feel angry and defensive, but reacting angrily or defensively is not going to be helpful.

When people you meet ask questions about your country, the best strategy is to answer such questions directly and seriously, no matter how ridiculous the question seems to you. It may be tempting to be sarcastic or to try turning the question around to make the person who asked it feel foolish, but why create bad feelings? That kind of response will not make you appear more intelligent—quite the contrary. The person who asked the question may not know much about your country now, but in some way you have sparked his or her interest and curiosity. You can help people become better informed if you do not discourage their questions.

Responding to criticism about your government or its national policies may be much more difficult. If you find that you don't know much about the particular issues raised, you may feel even more defensive. It is easy to feel that you are being personally criticized, as Holly did. However, this is unlikely to be the motive behind the comments made. Try to think instead of the reaction you would have if you heard the criticism from someone in your own country. This might help you see the criticism as less personal. Above all, avoid responding by criticizing the government of your host country. Instead, explain to the person that you have a different perspective. This may be enough of a response in itself or you may want to try to explain your own thoughts on the topic. It may be that the person was simply trying to learn your opinion.

Sometimes your role as an exchange student in the community can overwhelm you. You may be asked to give speeches to schools and organizations, so many that you seem to have little time left to spend with family and friends. Your schoolwork may take you much longer than other students because you are studying in a foreign language. The attempt to act the part of the perfect exchange student or the perfect "junior ambassador" can be exhausting. You need time to just be yourself and not always on display. Normally, your family and the program sponsors can help you drop some of these additional burdens if you explain your situation to them. You should not try to be heroic by doing more than is reasonable.

Being an exchange student *does* mean sharing yourself with people. It is important to remember that you don't have to become someone other than who you are. The role you play in the family and the community is unique, and you and your unique personality have a large part in creating it. Another exchange student may be excellent in sports, but you don't have to be. Another student may be a good public speaker; this doesn't mean that you must be. You have your own special strengths and these should determine what role you want to fulfill. It is only by following this guideline that you can find a way to best fit in the host community and create a role that is right for you.

2

What Does the Host Family Offer?

Host families are people who generously offer to open their lives and their homes to young people from other countries. Because there are many different types of families who host, it is difficult to describe exactly what your experience will be. Much depends on the particular characteristics of your family. Some families have many children, some have none. You may have two host parents or you may live in a single-parent home. Some are very orderly and their homes will always be kept neat. Others have a more relaxed attitude about neatness. The exchange organization has tried to place you in a family that can meet your individual needs, yet inevitably that family will be different from your own family in many important ways.

Living with a host family is an exciting and challenging way to discover a new country and culture. As an exchange student, you have the chance to join in the daily life of a family and a community of friends. How much more exciting and demanding than simply visiting a country's tourist sites! In living with a family you will be able to learn the language and come to understand the culture and way of life of your host country in much the same way that you learned your own language and absorbed and came to understand your own culture.

In your pursuit of this learning, your family will try to give you help and advice similar to the sort that your own family has given you over the years. They will want to help you feel comfortable in their home and in their country and will be ready to answer your questions and guide you (most of the time) when you feel unsure or confused.

But just as you are not a highly trained diplomat, neither are the members of your host family. They are probably not very knowledgeable about your country and the way of life there. They will not always treat you as you want to be treated. Sometimes your behavior may surprise or even shock them because it is so different from what they expect. They may also do things at times that shock you.

Differences don't necessarily mean problems. Both you and your host family will need to make adjustments in order to live together comfortably, but for most exchange students and their families, these adjustments can be made without serious difficulties. Generally it is the exchange student who must change his or her behavior. But members of the family, too, alter their lives in both large and small ways to accommodate you. In an unusual case, the teenaged boy in a host family decided to give his bedroom to the exchange student and made his own sleeping space in a small hallway in their home. More typical was Mary, who shared her room with Jacqueline from France. Whereas before Jacqueline's arrival, Mary had been used to some privacy and late hours reading or listening to music, now she needed to take Jacqueline's needs into consideration and turn out the lights or the music when Jacqueline wanted to sleep. Though you may share a room, you may not otherwise be aware of some of the changes the family makes for your benefit. Yet every family makes some changes in lifestyle in order to provide a comfortable place for their guest to sleep, dress, bathe, and study. Host families also adjust the patterns of their daily lives to meet the needs and demands of the student. Many try to help the exchange student feel more at home by buying some special foods from the student's home country. Your hosts may drive you to events or activities that you want to attend, even though it may interfere with other things that they'd like to do.

Not all changes constitute a sacrifice on the part of the host family, of course. The student typically adds a positive element to the family's life. You may give them a new way of looking at the world, bring them new music, new ideas, or different perspectives on how people relate to each other. Life for the family may become more fun, with more laughter, more conversation, and warmer interactions. Most families find that the changes a foreign family member brings into their lives are enriching rather than burdensome. As one host mother reported, "I tell everyone I meet, 'You should really treat yourself to this experience.' This has been the best year of my life. Our home feels more complete now. I have had fewer headaches this year. Our exchange student has brought so much happiness into our lives."

Lifestyle Sharing. Though it is seldom stated, families want to host exchange students because they want to share their lives with someone else. Most families feel good about their lifestyle and want the exchange student to join in it and enjoy being part of it. They want to explain their values and ideas and want you to understand them and the way they live. The best way you can do this is to participate in their lives as much as possible. Try to understand and appreciate their values even if you have different ones. Show an interest in their activities. Ask them about their ideas and opinions and listen to their answers. In doing this, you'll show your hosts that you accept and understand them.

You probably want to share your lifestyle with the host family as well, to tell them about your ideals and values, and talk to them about your way of life and the things that are important to you or that you enjoy doing. This doesn't mean that you compare your life to theirs as if it were a competition. If you are genuinely interested in knowing your host family and understanding their way of life, they'll most likely want to know more about you and will give you the same acceptance and understanding that you have shown them. Lifestyle sharing is extremely rewarding to both the family and the exchange student. By becoming involved in the life of your host family, you'll gain new insights on your own lifestyle and values.

Sam's Brazilian host family ran a small pharmacy in the store below their apartment. At first, he didn't pay much attention to the store. He had always seen his own parents' work as something that didn't concern him, and he had seldom seen their offices. But Sam soon started visiting the store after school. He began to ask questions about the business and helped out where he could by stocking the shelves. Eventually he got to know the customers who came in and could enjoy the amusing stories his host father often told about them. One time, a British customer came into the store who did not know Portuguese. Sam was able to help the man explain his problem and get the proper medication. The experience made Sam feel good about getting involved in the family's pharmacy. He felt that he belonged. He became curious about his own parents' occupations and how they might feel about their work. He also thought more about his own future career and realized that it was important to him to provide a useful service to the community, even if he didn't make lots of money.

Sometimes you may feel that your vocabulary is too small to express some of your ideas, feelings, or hopes for the future. Don't be discouraged. The rewards for your efforts will be great. Some exchange students bring things with them to share and to help them communicate with their hosts. A girl from the U.S. brought her host family a cassette tape of an American singer whose music she had found moving and important to her life. In fractured German, she tried to explain her feelings about the singer to her Austrian hosts. They were extremely pleased, even though they weren't quite sure what the American was trying to express in words. Seeing their response and hearing the music fill her hosts' home helped make the student feel accepted and appreciated by the family.

Gifts with special, personal meaning are not always given immediately upon arrival. Many students like to wait until they begin to feel close to their host families before they give them these things. A Chilean girl brought some of her favorite photos of herself and her family to give to her hosts. But it was almost three months before she brought them out. When she did, she recounted several stories about her childhood which related to the photos. While her relationship with the family had been good from the start, this personal gesture took the relationship to a deeper level of understanding and closeness. Lifestyle sharing often involves giving gifts. The best gifts to give are not those that are expensive or lavish, but those things that have personal meaning for you.

Support and Advice. During your stay in the host country, you may get help from your classmates and teachers, and possibly from other exchange students, but you will probably depend most on your host family for support and advice . Your host parents are responsible for your safety and well-being and will do everything they can to ensure your successful adjustment. Don't be afraid to ask them for help. Some students are too timid to ask questions because they do not want to appear stupid, or because they think their questions will be troublesome or embarrassing to their hosts. But embarrassment soon disappears, and your family will be much more upset with you if you do things that are inappropriate than if you ask a few questions that seem troublesome. This was certainly true in the case of one Indonesian boy who could not discover how to turn off the lamp in his bedroom. Because he did not want to ask his hosts to show him how, he left it on all night the entire first week that he stayed in their home. As a result, he did not sleep well and his host parents, when they found out about it, were annoyed about the wasted electricity.

Your host brothers or sisters can also be extremely helpful to you, especially in school and among young people in the community. It is not easy to establish new friendships when all the people your age have known each other for a long time. If you sometimes feel ignored and excluded, you can seek help from your host brothers or sisters. They may enjoy introducing you to their friends and helping you feel part of the group. Although eventually you will probably find your own group of friends, your host brothers and sisters should continue to be important sources of information and support.

You may decide that you can easily find your own friends and don't need any help from your family. But no matter how capable and mature you are at home, you do not always have all the information you need to make good decisions when living in another culture. As Maria, an Italian girl, learned, the host family's advice can sometimes keep you out of trouble.

> At first I thought that my host parents were interfering too much with my life. When I was going to a party or out with friends, they always wanted to know who the people were. I was really upset one time when they told me not to go to a

party that some boys at school were having. Even my host sister said I should stay away, and I couldn't understand why. Later I found out that the boys had a reputation for having parties where drugs and alcohol were used heavily and had been in trouble with the police several times.

There will be many times when you won't ask about something because you don't realize you need to. Julia, an American girl in Colombia, liked going around the house barefooted. In the U.S. what you wear or don't wear on your feet inside the house is a matter of personal preference. In California where she lived, going bare-footed is especially common. She didn't realize that, in Colombia, customs are more formal in regard to bare feet and that she was expected to keep her shoes or slippers on in the house. She was confused and insulted when her host family complained about it.[1] This and other assumptions about proper behavior are part of the "cultural baggage" that this girl brought with her when she left home. In the next chapter we will explore these assumptions further.

---

[1] See Raymond Gorden's book, *Living in Latin America* (Skokie, IL: National Textbook Company, 1974), 60-61.

3

Cultural Baggage:
Beyond the Customs Counter

Have you thought about what you are bringing with you when you leave home? Of course you have considered what clothes to pack and what gifts to bring to your hosts. Maybe you have also thought about books, games, musical instruments, or other items that you might want or need while you're abroad. But if you are like most people, you've probably never considered the cultural baggage that you will carrying along.

Cultural baggage is not something that you can see. It is not the kind of baggage that can be stored, checked at the airport, or conveniently left behind. It is a set of assumptions and values that you share with everyone else in your culture. Because almost everyone you know at home holds these same assumptions and beliefs about right and wrong, you probably take these things for granted and hardly realize that they exist. These cultural assumptions and values that you carry with you are like the air you breathe or the muscles you use to walk. Under ordinary circumstances, you don't notice them at all. But when you go to another culture where people share a different set of assumptions and values, you become acutely aware of them or at least you become aware that something is wrong.

How does this happen? Your reactions to the situations and people you meet will be based largely on your assumptions about how people behave and what that behavior means. Let's look at some examples. Think about what your reactions would be to the following situations:

1. Your host sister talks to her cat and kisses it.
2. Your host sister wears the same clothes several days in a row.

3. The boys in your host school talk about sports and cars and show little interest in politics.
4. Your host family holds hands and prays before meals.
5. While walking in the park, you see several couples lying on the ground, kissing.
6. Students in your school are not allowed to wear any makeup or jewelry even outside of school.
7. Your host parents and sisters go up to their bedroom right after dinner and spend the evening there watching TV.

It is likely that some situations in this list seem ordinary to you. Others will seem strange or maybe even shocking. Your assumptions about what is normal and what is unacceptable behavior are securely packed in your cultural baggage. What you carry in this baggage will not work in your host country because many of your assumptions and values do not apply there. You will need to watch what others do, ask questions, and withhold making judgments until you know more. Let's take the examples above and see how the wrong assumptions can disrupt a relationship.

1. **Your host sister talks to her cat and kisses it.**
Mary, a girl from Kenya, could not believe the way her American host sister, Elizabeth, treated the cat. One morning, the two of them were sitting quietly over breakfast at the kitchen table, when the cat walked into the kitchen. Elizabeth picked the cat up, kissed him several times, held him like a baby, and talked to him in a silly baby style, saying things like, "Well, hello kitty! Is he our adorable kitty? Yes he is. Does Mr. Kitty want some breakfast?" Mary was so disgusted she could hardly eat. She could not believe that Elizabeth would kiss that dirty cat and bring him so close to the breakfast table. Even worse, she seemed to pay more attention to the cat than she did to Mary.

The host sister's behavior with her cat is common in the United States. Many people are very affectionate with their pets and talk to them often in a kind of baby talk. Of course, they know the animals do not understand the words, but the animals seem to respond to the tone of human voices. Elizabeth would believe that a house cat is a very clean animal and would not worry about keeping the cat away from her food. But talking to the cat also helps ease Elizabeth's discomfort with the lack of conversation at the table. On that particular day, Elizabeth and Mary were eating silently, because neither could think of anything to say. Mary didn't notice the silence particularly, but for Elizabeth, the silence was very awkward, so she was especially glad when the cat came into the room and she could break the silence by fussing over him a little. Had Mary been an American girlfriend, she might have also used the entrance of the cat as a way to start a new conversation, with a comment such as, "He reminds me of a cat our neighbors had."

Mary could break the cycle of misunderstanding by asking Elizabeth about her attitude toward cats. She might simply say, "I never saw anyone kiss a cat before." Elizabeth might be a little surprised, and curious, about Kenya. She would probably tell Mary that many Americans love cats and treat them like this. She would probably begin to ask Mary some questions about life in Kenya, and there would be a good start in building a closer relationship between the two girls.

2. **Your host sister wears the same clothes several days in a row.**

Lisa was an American girl in a small German town. She brought two large suitcases filled with clothes. She also brought the assumption in her cultural baggage that she would need all those clothes in order to be accepted in her host school. When she noticed that Tina, her host sister, had worn the same clothes to school for several days in a row, Lisa began to wonder about her host family's social or economic status. They *seemed* to be well-off enough to afford to buy more clothes for their daughter, but perhaps they weren't. Or maybe Tina was just sloppy about her personal hygiene, which was worse. She worried that Tina might not be popular at school and might not be able to introduce her to the right crowd.

In some cultures it is simply logical to wear the same outfit as long as it remains basically clean and is appropriate to the occasion. In the U.S., however, women (and men too) generally expect to change the clothes they wear every day, especially if they will be among the same people. They want to have clothes enough to wear something different every day of the week. In U.S. high schools, clothes are frequently a measure of social status. In these circumstances, wearing the same outfit twice in a row suggests an inability to afford appropriate clothing—or personal sloppiness. If Lisa had spent less time worrying about her social status and being accepted by the right people and more time observing how the other girls in the school dressed (it was common for them to wear the same clothes on successive days)—in other words, if she had focused on what it meant to *them* rather than what it meant to her, she would have taken a valuable step in unloading some of the burden of her cultural baggage.

3. **The boys in your host school talk about sports and cars and show little interest in politics.**
   Jonas, a Danish boy, wanted to learn more about U.S. foreign policy and hoped to engage in vigorous discussions about politics with his new American friends the way he did with his intelligent Danish friends at home. Instead, he found himself bored in conversations that revolved only around football (an American sport that he did not understand), cars, and rock music. He couldn't believe how little the boys in his school knew about their own country's government and foreign policy. While many of them seemed intelligent, their inability to discuss politics indicated the opposite.

   It is generally true that American teenagers seldom get into heavy intellectual debates about politics. One reason for this is that politics and religion are considered sensitive conversational subjects by most Americans. Discussions about politics or religion have the potential for creating controversy which can threaten social ties between people. They will be avoided except where those involved in the conversation essentially agree with or are well known to one another. So safe topics of conversation include such things as sports and cars, movies and television programs, and sharing stories about situations at school, home, or work. Jonas might find out that conversations about such seemingly trivial matters can be fun. He might also learn about politics in the United States by asking questions about the political system rather than trying to argue about opinions. Many of the students who don't want to debate U.S. foreign policy may actually know quite a bit about national and local issues and various federal, state, and local laws that affect them and their families. He will find that Americans are willing to explain their views to those who are not trying to argue against them.

4. Your host family holds hands and prays before meals.

Dieter, a German boy, did not believe in God and so felt it would be dishonest for him to pray. He was shocked when the family sat down for dinner on his first night there, held hands, and began to pray about him. The family thanked God for his safe arrival at their home. In Dieter's view it was not God who brought him there, and he refused to participate further in the ceremony.

Many families in the United States customarily offer family prayers before meals as a way of reaffirming their basic religious beliefs. Some hold hands as part of this prayer because it gives them a feeling of closeness as a family. Guests are typically included in the prayers and welcomed into the family circle in this way. Dieter felt that the prayer forced him to participate in a religion in which he did not believe, whereas the family sought only to welcome him in a manner that fit their beliefs without forcing these upon him. Dieter needed to postpone evaluating the event until it became clearer what the meaning of the prayer was.

5. While walking in the park, you see several couples lying on the ground, kissing.

Mui-Ying, a Chinese girl, went to the park in an American city on Saturday afternoon with some new friends from her school. At first she liked the park and enjoyed being with her new friends. However, before long she noticed three or four couples who were lying on the ground and kissing each other, even with everyone in the park watching. She decided that these must be prostitutes with their clients and was angry that her friends would bring her to such an unsafe neighborhood.

On warm days in U.S. cities, young couples often go to the park to relax and be together. Even though they are in a public place, it is unlikely that anyone will pay much attention to a couple if they decide to lie down on the grass or kiss each other. Anyone who happens to notice will soon look away and walk on. Rather than becoming upset, Mui-Ying might have withheld judgment based on the meaning of this kind of behavior in her own society and instead simply asked her friends what they thought about the couples. They would have told her that it is not uncommon for American couples to lie on the grass and kiss in public places and reassured her that she was perfectly safe.

6. Students in your host school are not allowed to wear any makeup or jewelry even outside of school.
Erica, a teenager from an American suburb, has worn earrings since she was eight years old, when she had her ears pierced. When she was eleven or twelve, she began to experiment with a wide assortment of makeup and hair coloring. Now makeup and jewelry were a normal part of her style of dress. When her Japanese host family forbade her to wear her makeup and jewelry, telling her the school would not allow it, she immediately called the exchange organization to demand a less conservative family.

Japanese high schools exercise strict control over students' dress and behavior both within and outside of class. At sixteen or seventeen years old, a Japanese girl is still considered too young to wear makeup and jewelry. Erica's family knew the problems their use could create in school and did not want her to be an outcast because of it. Erica reacted too quickly to a situation she did not understand and found difficult to accept. As the exchange organization advised her, she should take more time to observe customs among Japanese girls her age. She would have found out that it was the custom in Japan for girls to put off wearing makeup and jewelry longer than girls do in the United States. She would also have learned something about the social mores and the orientation toward academic studies which prevail in the Japanese school system. This kind of learning was, after all, among the principal reasons for her becoming an exchange student in the first place.

7. **Your host parents and sisters go up to their bedroom right after dinner and spend the evening there watching TV.**

   Steve, a boy from the United States, wanted to spend time with his host family, but every night the parents and sisters went to the parents' bedroom immediately after dinner. Assuming they wanted some private time as a family, since they didn't stay downstairs in the living room, he passed the time alone in his bedroom, reading and writing letters. He felt odd staying by himself in the living room in any case. He could hear the television in the parents' bedroom, and he wished he had a television in his room, too. Steve had wanted to live with a family to get to know the Colombian way of life. He didn't want to live as a boarder. He wished they would sometimes stay downstairs with him in the living room. He wondered if they were unhappy with him. Maybe they were trying to avoid him.

   In Colombian families the living room is often reserved for more formal entertaining, while the television tends to be in the parents' bedroom. The family will typically gather in this room in the evenings to watch television or socialize. Family friends may also be entertained in the bedrooms. When Steve isolated himself in his bedroom, the host parents assumed he needed time to study and wanted to be alone. Steve let his shyness and insecurity interfere with what he really wanted to do—be with his hosts. He needed to let his hosts know that he would enjoy spending time with them after dinner. He would have quickly learned that the bedroom was not off-limits to him.

In each of these cases, the exchange students' cultural baggage caused them to make inappropriate assumptions about the behavior of their friends or their host families. Mary assumed that her host sister's open (and strange) affection for her pet animal was unhealthy and inappropriate. Lisa assumed that her host sister's wearing the same clothes several days in a row reflected either on her host sister's personal habits or the social status of her family. She also assumed that, in Germany as in the United States, popularity in school can be influenced by how you dress. Jonas assumed that because a sign of intelligence in Denmark is the ability to argue knowledgeably about politics, his friends in the U.S. were less intelligent because they avoided political discussions. Rather than attempt to learn what prayer at mealtimes means in American culture, Dieter assumed that his host family was trying to impose their religious beliefs on him. Mui-Ying assumed that lying on the ground kissing is as improper for Americans as it is for Chinese. Erica misjudged her family because she assumed that social mores in Japanese schools were the same as in the U.S., and Steve was unable to spend evenings with his host family because he assumed that bedrooms were strictly private places as they are in his own home.

You cannot prepare yourself for every situation you will face, nor can you entirely avoid misunderstandings. But you can be ready to clear up misunderstandings by remembering that your cultural baggage contains assumptions that do not apply in your host country.

4

What You Need to Know about Culture

In the English language, the word "culture" can have several different meanings. When you think of culture, perhaps you think of art, ballet, and music. Perhaps you think of traditional costumes and crafts. In this book, culture has a much broader meaning. It is the patterns of thought and behavior that are collectively established in each society. It includes the way you automatically respond to stories, events, other people, or situations that you face. In most cases, you are not aware of these patterns of culture because they are natural to you. When we think about culture in this way, we sometimes call it "deep culture" because it concerns knowledge that is deep in the mind, outside of a person's awareness.

Deep culture is learned by you as a child and includes everything you need to know to live, work, make friends, and be part of your cultural group. It consists of the unwritten rules that guide your behavior and the way you look at the world. It is the answer your culture provides for such questions as:

- When is it acceptable to tell a lie, and to whom?
- Under what circumstances can you visit another person's home?
- What sorts of questions are too personal to ask?
- What obligations do you have toward your parents or toward your brother or sister?
- What sort of people do you avoid?
- What sort of relationship do you establish with your neighbors?

Though people from the same culture may not always answer these sorts of questions in the same way, people from different cultures answer such questions very differently and have different explanations for the answers they give. Let's take the last question. For many Americans, it is important to establish good relationships with neighbors, since these are the people who are physically closest to you and on whom you may need to rely in an emergency. American neighbors may borrow sugar or milk, lend tools, watch each other's children, or look after each other's property or pets when one is on vacation, building up a relationship of trust and mutual help. In France, this question would be answered quite differently. Being geographically close is not a strong enough basis for a relationship, so there is not a general pattern of neighborliness as there is in the U.S.[1] Instead, one depends on family and friends for some of the help often provided by American neighbors. Indeed, in France, family would likely be living close by and could easily provide the assistance necessary.

People who have only lived in one culture are usually not aware that people in other cultures have other ways of thinking. Such things as logic and truth have different meanings and values in different cultures. What is viewed as right in one society may be wrong in another. Each culture has its own ideas of how to care for children, to make friends, to start conversations, to buy and sell goods, or to reach decisions within a group. In India, strangers often start conversations by asking questions about the other's family: How many brothers and sisters do you have? Are you married? How many children do you have? How old are you? For an American, this kind of question arouses suspicion and perhaps anger: My personal life is none of your business!

When you enter an unfamiliar culture, you do not have all this knowledge. To survive, you will need to learn at least some of it; the more you learn of the other culture the better you will be able to take part in it. Acquiring another culture's knowledge is not as simple as learning its history or geography. The knowledge of deep culture is taught to each generation from infancy. Over the years of growing up in your own family and community, you have learned meanings and values that are deeply rooted in your ways of thinking and patterns of behavior. By the time you are sixteen or seventeen years old, you probably know most of what you need to know to participate in your own society. However, to participate in a new and different society, you will have to learn new meanings and new ways of behaving. This is more complex than simply learning to use a fork instead of chopsticks. Because it is based on assumptions that you don't think about very much at home (they are, after all, the same assumptions everyone else has), your behavior will be different from that of the people in the host country.

Although you may not immediately recognize the ways in which your deep culture differs from that of your host country, there are techniques you can use to help you see these differences.

Red Flags. It was Professor Elijah Lovejoy, of the University of California at Santa Barbara, who first suggested the idea of looking for "red flags" when visiting another culture.[2] Red flags are simply your own reactions to the host culture. The technique is to use these reactions to warn you of deep-culture differences that could lead to misunderstanding. Exchange students frequently react to the host culture by thinking: "These people are rude," or "They are stupid." It is probably not possible to avoid such reactions. However, instead of letting them stop communication, reactions can be turned into red flags to remind you that a different way of thinking exists in the deep culture of your host country. Cathy, from the U.S., went to the bank in India to cash traveler's checks. Several people were ahead of her at the counter, so she stood behind them waiting to be served. Finally she felt it was her turn. But before she could get a chance to cash her check, a man came in and shoved his check under the teller's window ahead of her. "How rude!" Cathy thought. When it happened a second time, though, she realized that this was a red-flag warning. At the same time, another man behind her helped her figure out what to do. He told her to move in close and to push her check right under the teller's window while someone else was being helped. In following his advice, she laughed to think that now she, too, was being "rude."

When you have a red-flag reaction, ask yourself: Are these

people actually being rude or do they have different rules for politeness? What is it about these people that makes them seem stupid to me?

Some positive reactions to the host culture can also be red flags. When they first arrive in the United States, many exchange students think: "These people are very friendly." In the U.S., being friendly is a customary pattern of behavior when people first meet a stranger. It doesn't mean they are ready to become close friends in a short time. Ivan, a Russian exchange student in the U.S., believed that he had quickly made a number of close friends among the Americans he first met. They invited him to come with them to a movie and then later they all went for hamburgers. It was lots of fun and they all laughed hard recalling scenes from the movie. He was surprised at how quickly and easily they included him in their circle. As the weeks went by, however, and these friends did not call him up or invite him to their homes, he realized that the surprise he felt at having made friends so quickly was in fact a red flag. Though they still said hello and seemed friendly when they saw him at school, the friendships did not become close. In fact, he realized that establishing friendships takes time in the U.S., just as it does in Russia, and what appeared to be close friendship was merely common courtesy. He could still become friends with these people, whom he liked, but it was going to take time and effort on his part.

Exchange students who adopt the red-flag technique will be able to use their own reactions as a way to learn about the host country's deep culture. The red flag will warn them to look for explanations for what they have noticed to be new or different from what they would expect at home.

Expectations. As Craig Storti points out in *The Art of Crossing Cultures*, much of the difficulty that people have in trying to live in another culture (and much of the fun as well) comes from the fact that they expect others to behave as *they* do, and these expectations aren't met.[3] John returned angry from his trip into the city. He complained to his host brother, Abdul, about the man who gave him the wrong directions and sent him some ten blocks out of his way. "If he didn't know where the museum was, why didn't he just say so?" asked John. If a foreigner showed up in John's hometown and asked him for directions, he would certainly never lie and give the wrong directions. But instead of sympathizing with him, Abdul told him he was foolish not to ask someone else. After all, not everyone could be expected to know where the museum was. He should have asked several people along the way. If he had done this, he would have saved a lot of trouble. Abdul's reaction to the story surprised John and made him even angrier. He could understand that they didn't know where it was, but why would they lie? "They're not lying; they're just being polite," Abdul explained. "You've asked them a question and they're giving you an answer."

When pressed, John had to admit that on certain occasions, he might also answer a question with polite "white lies." But the occasions were different. In the U.S., he expected people he asked to tell him that they liked his new haircut or sweater, even if they didn't. Here in Egypt, those asking for directions expect people to give them some, even if they don't know the way. Though he was initially angry, he now realized that it was his *expectations* that were wrong, not the person who gave him the wrong directions.

Describe, Interpret, Evaluate. Shortly after he arrived in India, Dan wrote home telling his parents how shocked he was at the way his host mother treated her youngest son. "He is spoiled rotten," he wrote. In *The Handbook of Foreign Student Advising*, Gary Althen talks about an orientation activity called the D.I.E. Formulation.[4] This is an exercise, originally formulated by Janet and Milton Bennett, which focuses on the distinctions among the three activities: Describing, Interpreting, and Evaluating. As Althen points out, most of the reactions people have, such as Dan's "their son was spoiled rotten" or one often made by Asian students on first entering class in the U.S., "the classroom was chaotic," are not descriptions of what people actually see, but are their interpretations of what they think they see and their evaluations about the situation. In Dan's case, a real description of what he saw might be as follows:

> When the mother tried to sit down at the table to eat, the son cried, "No! Don't eat now. Play with me." She left her dinner and sat down with her son to play with him until he was somewhat distracted, at which point she got up and returned to the table, only to have him call out again to her to play with him. This happened several times.

When Dan says that the boy is spoiled, he is interpreting what he observed; when he says he is spoiled *rotten*, he is evaluating this behavior as something negative and to be avoided. Dan and his host mother might agree on the description above, since it is essentially factual. The mother may or may not agree with the interpretation that she is spoiling the boy. But she would surely disagree that there was anything rotten about it, since her behavior is normal in Indian society. Her husband and brothers were brought up with similar indulgence, and they have turned out to be mature, responsible, and caring men.

You can avoid some misunderstandings if you are careful to describe the behavior you see rather than interpreting it or evaluating it from the perspective of your own cultural context.

Attributions and Stereotypes. We often explain behavior by identifying its causes. When we explain our own behavior, we are likely to attribute it to the particular situation in which we find ourselves. Suppose I am quiet one day during a discussion. I might explain my being quiet by saying that I was tired that day or that I did not have enough information to participate. If others were to explain my behavior, however, they might say that I am a quiet person. They would not be as likely to consider the situation I am facing, but would attribute the behavior to a personality characteristic.

In a cross-cultural setting, attributions result in stereotypes that may offer a false explanation for individual behavior. Stereotypes are oversimplified judgments made about people on the basis of their cultural group or physical characteristics. Cultural stereotypes may be quite strong and will not disappear easily. Tourists, in their brief contact with another country, often find confirmation of the stereotypes they hold.[5] Exchange students have a better chance to understand the host culture than the typical tourist, yet they, too, may find their stereotypes confirmed by their experiences there. Though there is often some generalized truth in stereotypes, real-life situations and the people who face them are more complex than the stereotype admits. So while a generalization can be made, for example, that Americans are concerned with time and being prompt, the stereotype of the American ruled by the clock is not accurate, and such a stereotype can interfere with forming friendships across cultures.

Elena's American host sister screamed at her one morning because they were running a few minutes late for school. Elena explained the host sister's behavior with a stereotype she held about North Americans: they are obsessed with the idea of being on time. Had she asked her host sister about her behavior, however, she would have heard a very different explanation. The host sister would have said that she was anxious about an important math test she was going to take that morning. She worried about getting to school late that day and missing the beginning of the test.

Because the Honduran girl attributed the behavior she saw to a stereotype of Americans, she wasn't interested in trying to understand the situation better, nor was she able to feel any sympathy for the concerns of her host sister about her math test. Elena already believed that people in the United States are obsessed with time, and her host sister's behavior only reinforced this stereotype. She learned nothing new about her host sister.

Being alert to your own attributions and stereotyping is one way to make certain that these simplified judgments do not interfere with the relationships you are trying to build. You can begin to recognize the stereotypes you have of the host culture even before you leave home. Think about the images you have of people from your host culture. Do you see them as wealthy? Lazy? Rigid? Warm? Formal? All of these images form the basis of stereotypes. By reminding yourself that these *are* stereotypes and, therefore, misleading, you may be better able to avoid allowing such images to influence your opinions and feelings about the people you meet. By reminding yourself that individual circumstances affect people's behavior, you may find it easier to search for other ways to explain the behavior of your hosts.

---

[1] See other examples of French and American cultural differences in *Cultural Misunderstandings: The French-American Experience*. Raymonde Carroll (Chicago: University of Chicago Press, 1988).

[2] A description of this technique can be found in Cornelius Grove, *Orientation Handbook for Youth Exchange Programs* (Yarmouth, ME: Intercultural Press, 1989), 149-56.

[3] Craig Storti, *The Art of Crossing Cultures* (Yarmouth, ME: Intercultural Press, 1989), 47 ff.

[4] Gary Althen, *The Handbook of Foreign Student Advising* (Yarmouth, ME: Intercultural Press, 1983), 143-4.

[5] See Philip L. Pearce, "Tourists and Their Hosts: Some Sociological and Psychological Effects of Inter-Cultural Contact," in Stephen Bochner, ed., *Cultures in Contact* (Oxford: Pergamon Press, 1982), 199-221.

5

The Adjustment Cycle

If you think about your life back home, you will undoubtedly remember days when everything seemed to go wrong and you felt pretty miserable. You'll also remember happy times, full of laughter and good friends, when life seemed wonderful, exciting, and new. Life as an exchange student is no different, except that when you are living in a foreign culture, the range of emotions may be wider and the feelings may be more intense because of the many differences you are encountering and the many changes and adaptations you are called upon to make. Your year abroad is not simply a long vacation in which your principal aim is to have as much fun as possible. It is, on the one hand, just another year in your life in which a variety of good and bad things will occur yet, on the other hand, a special year of learning and growth, which can be taxing, stressful, and even painful at times.

Though every exchange student has a different set of experiences, some are fairly common and occur in some form in the exchange experience of most students. The result is a general pattern of emotional ups and downs over the year. This pattern is called "the adjustment cycle." Your particular pattern of adjustment may not follow this cycle precisely. You may meet with different experiences at different times and you may react differently to them. Still, it is useful to explore and understand what the adjustment cycle is because it can help explain many things that happen to you even though they don't fit the exact pattern described in the cycle. In particular, understanding the ups and downs that most exchange students go through can reassure you that your own feelings are normal and appropriate.

Even before leaving your home country you may alternate between feeling excited and worried, between feeling happy about the coming year and sad about leaving your family and friends. Maybe you're mostly feeling confused and can't believe you're really going abroad. Such fluctuations will continue throughout the year in ways that are often predictable. In this chapter, we will describe briefly the kinds of events and experiences that are likely to affect the way you feel at particular stages during the exchange year. Later chapters will discuss these stages in more detail and offer practical advice for coping with the situations you will meet.

ARRIVAL FATIGUE

For some exchange students, arrival in the host country is unbelievably exciting. It is the fulfillment of a dream they have had for a long time. There is the thrill of travel, of meeting the host family, and of seeing so many new sights. In the words of one exchange student, "All my life I had dreamed about the United States. I couldn't believe that I was actually there. I was really talking in English with people at the airport. The stores, the cars, the people—I loved everything immediately."

For other students, anxiety may be stronger than excitement. They may start their experience with thoughts that they should not have come. These students may be more worried about the experience, perhaps because they are better able to anticipate the discomfort they will feel at times during their exchange program.

In either case, soon after their arrival students are frequently exhausted by all the activity they find in their new surroundings. There are so many new people to meet, new places to go, and new things to do that they run out of energy and find that they can't continue to participate with enthusiasm. There is an additional problem of trying to speak and understand a new language. Some students arrive in their host country knowing very little of the language, but even those who have studied it before will become fatigued when they have to use it continually. During this period, exchange students often find themselves exhausted when they have to carry on a conversation of any length.

This arrival fatigue is brief for some; for others it may last several weeks or more. The length will depend upon the ease of the relationship with the host family, the student's ability in the language, and other factors, such as how soon school begins after the student's arrival.

HOMESICKNESS

It is not unusual for students to feel a little homesick soon after their arrival in a new country. This may happen because you are alone and in a strange place. "For the first time I was alone with my suitcase in the room that was to be my bedroom for the next year, and nothing in the room felt like home to me. I broke down in tears. I missed my family and my own home terribly just then." But the familiar can also bring on homesickness, as was the case with another student who became homesick when she heard a song that reminded her of her friends back home.

Episodes of homesickness don't have to be a serious problem for exchange students. Your room will become more homey and familiar as you unpack your things and arrange them as you like them. When you are busy and with your new friends, you won't have time to be homesick. And if every once in a while you feel a sharp longing to be back home, this doesn't mean that you are unhappy in your new surroundings.

Homesickness becomes a problem, however, when you romanticize home and start believing that everything at home is better than it is where you are. Those who constantly judge their host country by the idealized images they have of home will make themselves as well as everyone around them miserable. They are also bound to be terribly disappointed once they return home and find that life there isn't perfect either.

If you feel homesick, concentrate on the things you like about being here and the fun you can have. Don't isolate yourself from the host family. Find some activities you enjoy and keep busy. Before you know it, the homesickness will pass.

SETTLING IN

Not everything in the host country will cause adjustment problems. Most students discover significant similarities between themselves and their hosts, and the differences they encounter tend to be interesting or exotic and don't cause problems, at least at first. This is sometimes called the "honeymoon" phase of cross-cultural adjustment because like newlyweds or new lovers, one only sees what is fascinating or charming in the other. Students almost always find some new food, new place, or new activity that they especially like. They meet people they enjoy being with. They even discover that they understand the language better than they thought they would, though speaking it may still require much concentration. The post-arrival fatigue disappears and they begin to feel confident about their ability to adjust.

Not all students have a comfortable settling-in period, and even those who are soon feeling comfortable in their new home will face occasional frustration and confusion. The difficulties students face in this period stem often from their expectations about the experience. Those who arrive expecting to have a glamorous adventure as an exchange student become quickly annoyed and discouraged by the ordinary nature of life with their host family. Some students believe they will be the center of attention in the new school. If this does not happen, they may be disappointed. Making friends outside of the host family is not always easy in the first weeks.

DEEPENING THE RELATIONSHIP

It is impossible for the exchange student and host family to avoid making some mistakes in developing their relationship with each other. These mistakes, however, should not prevent them from becoming close. Students and their families may need to try different ways of relating to each other before they find a deep, strong understanding developing between them. The efforts made in these early weeks are well worth it.

This is also the time in which families and students must deal with many basic issues and rules that govern family life. Exchange students may not understand these rules, which are often different from the ones in their own families. Sometimes they do not believe the host-family rules are serious. "Why are these things so important to them?" the exchange student may ask. "Why must I shake hands with my host parents?" was the question one American student asked about her French family. An Irish boy wondered, "How can it possibly matter how I fold my towel?" A Chinese girl asked her American friend, "Is it true that I must keep my mouth closed when I eat?"

The rules the family sets are rooted in the values of the host culture. Since the exchange student is unfamiliar with these values, following the family rules will not always feel natural. As the relationship with the family deepens, the exchange student will understand better what the family expects of their members. He or she will feel more comfortable with the rules they set and will begin to feel more a part of the family's life.

This is typically the stage at which a student will stop being a houseguest. A former student advises, "You can't expect them to keep on entertaining you, taking you places, or making a point to introduce you to new people. You also have something to give: you have your culture, your ideas, and your perspectives on the world. And you need to be interested in *them* and their ideas, also." By living together on an everyday basis, and learning about each other, exchange students and their families can develop and deepen a satisfying relationship.

CULTURE SHOCK

In the early weeks of the program, exchange students may be only slightly aware of the differences between their home and host cultures. Of course, they will immediately notice the obvious differences, such as the language and food. For most students, adjustments to these basic aspects of society don't interfere with their ability to function effectively. Most exchange students are eager to try the new things and test their skill in the foreign language. But as time passes, the eagerness to try new things wears off, and many students long for something familiar. They may now understand the language better, but be confused by what people say to them. In the first days of Yoko's stay in the United States, she didn't understand much of anything said to her, but she was eager to learn English and worked steadily to improve her vocabulary. She made rapid progress so that by four weeks into her stay, she had almost no trouble making herself understood and in understanding what people said to her. But now, though she understood what was said, she always had to stop to think about what sort of response was expected of her. How much easier it would have been to have a group of her Japanese friends to talk with. Then she would have known what to say. Now she could only sit silently and uncomfortably. She was becoming acutely aware that Americans think and behave differently than Japanese.

The feelings of confusion about the host culture can sometimes be so uncomfortable for an exchange student that he or she will experience what is known as "culture shock." Culture shock often includes actual physical problems such as headaches, stomachaches, inability to sleep, and loss of appetite. Students experiencing culture shock sometimes cry easily or may be quick to feel angry. They may be forgetful or develop mild obsessions with such things as cleanliness or orderliness. Culture shock is a normal reaction to the extreme stress and confusion that people often feel when trying to adapt to living in a foreign culture.

Like most students, Yoko's discomfort did not become severe. At first her frustration at being unable to participate comfortably in conversations made her want to shut herself up in her room and hide. She worried that she wasn't succeeding as an exchange student. She noticed a rash developing on her hands and face, though she knew it was just from nervousness. The best response to these kinds of problems is to find someone who will be a friend and who can help. Yoko did not have to look very far to find someone who cared about her. Linda, her host sister, was a very kind person who went out of her way to try to make Yoko feel wanted and at home. Yoko noticed small kindnesses, like the time when she was watching TV by herself and Linda came out to join her carrying mugs of hot chocolate for both of them. In some ways, Linda's behavior seemed very Japanese. Yoko found she could talk with Linda when they were alone. She remained shy in groups for a long time, but being able to talk with at least one person made her less anxious and frustrated. Though she still sat silently most of the time, she was not really uncomfortable—most Japanese are comfortable with silence—and she stopped being troubled by rashes.

Though some students suffer more with culture shock than others do, all exchange students face new circumstances and challenges that can be difficult and upsetting. Some of these come very early in the experience. Often, students do not recognize the most profound cultural differences until somewhat later in their year, when they are beginning to learn and understand more. These differences can be the most difficult and bring on a more intense feeling of culture shock than some of the earlier experiences. There are five basic dimensions to culture shock at this stage that affect most students in some measure. These fundamental dimensions are described below.

Identity. In the U.S., Rachel felt pretty confident of her identity. She knew what she believed, knew what type of person she was, and understood how she fit into her culture and society. Here's how she described herself on the application forms provided by the exchange organization:

> I'm an active person and am always doing something or, more often, several things. I belong to three or four clubs at school as well as the student government, so I'm always busy with activities and meetings after school.

Like many Americans, Rachel describes who she is by talking about what she does. She is active, involved, busy. But after several weeks in India, she realizes that this description no longer works. Who is she? According to her hosts, "She comes from a well-educated family. Her father is a businessman, and her older brother is studying medicine." This was certainly true, but what did it say about her? She knew little enough about business or medicine. But neither could she continue to think of herself as very active or involved. It seemed that she was spending most of her time in the house with her host mother and sister and the grandmother who lived with them. Had she suddenly become a homebody—someone who does nothing but stay at home?

Rachel is still the same person she always was in many ways, but her confusion about her identity in India stems from basic differences in cultural roles, values, and behaviors. In the United States, Rachel is identified according to her role as a student and her involvement in high school clubs and activities. When she is introduced to new people, she is likely very early in the meeting to tell them what school she attends, because this helps identify her to the other person. Her status within the school is measured in part by her involvement in school clubs and government, which are seen as her individual achievements. In American society, club and student-government involvement are given important consideration in many job and college applications. Personal achievement is a common standard for judging a person. There are also less tangible rewards for Rachel's involvement and activity, including the esteem of her classmates, her teachers, and her parents. Rachel thinks of herself as active because this is important in American society. In India, a person's family relationships are critical. You can't really know a person if you know nothing about his or her family. The people Rachel meets in India don't know her family, so her hosts are quick to help them fill in the missing pieces of Rachel's identity. What is important about Rachel in India is the status of her father and brother and her closeness to her family. Rachel's new behavior—staying home with the host family—reflects the importance of the family in a person's identity. Staying home is reinforced by the society in which she now lives.

Your identity is who you are as an individual, but also as part of the culture and society to which you belong. Other people from your culture identify you by your position in that culture and expect you to behave in certain ways according to the role or position you have. Your culture may have expectations for you as the oldest child, as the daughter, or as a member of a certain social class or religious group. When you live in another culture as an exchange student, you may suddenly find that your position in the society is seen quite differently, and different behavior may be called for.

Like Rachel, you are likely to find that your old image of yourself is threatened, changed, or possibly even shattered. As you develop a new image, you find it does not exactly match your old one. Becoming a different person in such a short time can be scary and stressful. As you discover the changes, you may wonder how much of that old image still really describes who you are. How much can you change and adapt and still be yourself?

If you stop to think about it, you may realize that you've gone through changes before. You may have asked yourself similar questions and had similar doubts about your identity at other times in your life, perhaps when you reached puberty, when you changed schools, when you lost a close friend, when your family moved, or when a family member died. Remembering how you came through those times before can be helpful to you now.

Dependence. As you have grown up, you have become more and more independent in your actions. Many things your parents used to do for you are things you can now handle easily on your own. Since you are leaving your family behind for a while, being an exchange student may seem to be another step toward independence. In some ways this is true, yet even for the most independent students, being an exchange student also means being *dependent* on others, especially at first. You may, for instance, need to depend on a member of your host family or find a friend to drive you where you want to go; in a similar situation at home, transportation would not have been a problem. You will also be more dependent in subtler ways. For example, you may be dependent on your family's advice about what clothes to wear for various occasions or what is appropriate to say or do in specific situations. You may feel the need to have someone around to "translate" jokes or stories that you don't understand. While being dependent in these ways is not always a problem, it may make you feel like a child again at a time in your life when you are eager to be treated as an adult.

Anger. Frustration and anger are typical reactions to the confusion of being in a new culture. Since you do not fully understand what is going on, you cannot foresee what will happen, and you are less in control of your circumstances than you would be at home. Your host family doesn't respond to you the way your own family does, so you can't predict how they will react at any given time. For example, they might laugh at some misfortune of yours instead of showing you the sympathy you hoped to get. Or, just the opposite, they may suddenly become upset and worried when you tell them about something funny that happened to you. For example, Simone, from France, was absolutely dumbfounded that her American parents were so disturbed about the telephone call she answered from some unknown man who, while breathing heavily, talked to her suggestively about sex. Simone thought it was quite a joke: what a stupid man! She laughed at him and told him that he was probably so ugly that no woman would want him. But her host parents seemed quite alarmed by the call and worried that the man would call back. They even considered how they might get the operator to trace the call, and they lectured Simone about how she should handle this type of call if she ever had one again.

There will be times when you tell your friends or family about something that happened to you and you won't get the reaction you expect. If this is a frequent occurrence, you may start to feel angry. It is especially important in cross-cultural adaptation to be able to deal with your disappointed expectations. You may feel rejected by your family or by your new friends who don't seem to understand you, and this, too, can make you angry.

You may also be frustrated by difficulties you're having in school. You may sometimes find yourself near tears when you don't understand what is going on in class. In such cases, your frustration may show up as anger toward the teachers or the other students, or even at yourself. If you are uncomfortable or fearful about trying something new, this, too, can make you react angrily. It is human to resist changes sometimes, and anger is a typical reaction to unwanted changes. But there is a positive side to this: When we are forced to make a change we did not want to make but which is called for by the circumstances of our lives, we often learn something new and may even come to prefer the new way of doing things.

Mourning. As a result of these kinds of changes, combined with the sadness you may feel about leaving your family and friends and the general homesickness you will almost certainly feel at times, you are likely to experience a period of grief or mourning. It is difficult to leave the old self behind and grow into a new, more mature person. You may miss the way you used to be, even while valuing what you have become.

Recovery. As time passes, you will be better able to deal with the differences you discover between home and host cultures. You learn more about them—yes, even when away from home you can learn about your own culture as it contrasts with the new one you are experiencing. You also learn new ways of behaving and new perspectives on life and the world around you. You enter a period of recovery from culture shock. At this point, you feel more confidence in yourself and your ability to function in your surroundings and to handle new challenges and problems.

THE HOLIDAYS

In every culture there are special holidays that are important family and community celebrations. When the host family celebrates a holiday that is new and unfamiliar to the exchange student, most find it easy to join in the celebration. Exchange students are sometimes more enthusiastic about the holiday than the host family, but it is more difficult for them to feel part of the gatherings of family and friends that often accompany a major holiday. When the discussion turns to memories of past holidays and old family stories, exchange students may feel left out and forgotten, since they had no part in these events.

Another sort of holiday experience, however, is when exchange students are staying in cultures where their own important holidays are not celebrated or are celebrated very differently. They frequently feel lonely and sad because they are missing an important occasion back home.

In the United States, the major holiday season begins in late November and continues through early January. This time of year brings as much tension and loneliness for some as it brings excitement for others.

CULTURE LEARNING

Once exchange students have recovered from culture shock and weathered the holidays, the confidence they have gained helps them face new challenges. At this point, they're ready to learn more about this new culture and way of life, and they're ready to learn more about themselves and their own culture as well. Though they may still feel some frustration, anger, or sadness from time to time, the difficulties of adjustment are generally past. Students who earlier resisted the unfamiliar experiences they were having are now better prepared to understand and accept new ideas and information. They can now bear some confusion and tolerate ambiguity and uncertainty, and their expectations are more realistic. Culture learning consists of being able to absorb the experience of a new culture and respond appropriately to it, evaluating it carefully, adapting as necessary, and adopting new ways of thinking and behaving that seem desirable. It involves being able to appreciate and value that which is different and people who are different, while at the same time reaffirming one's own individual and cultural identity.

Some students complain of boredom during this time, though probably no more than they would in their home countries. They may argue with their host brothers and sisters, or they may do things that anger their host families at times. This may simply be a sign that they feel accepted by their hosts. They don't feel the need to be so polite and careful about their behavior now. This is part of developing close familylike relationships which can be rich and rewarding to both the exchange students and their hosts.

Culture learning builds on these two basic factors: the confidence that students now have to try something new and the special insight that they gain through the growing relationships with their families and friends. At this stage, they are really participating in the culture, not just observing it. They are learning by doing rather than being taught.

PREDEPARTURE

In the weeks before the student's return home, feelings are almost always mixed. Confusion is again normal. While students are excited about the prospect of seeing their own families and friends again, it is difficult to leave their new family and friends in the host country. In addition, many students are suddenly inundated by invitations to parties and special activities scheduled for the end of the school year. These events and the conflicting emotions they stir up leave many students feeling exhausted.

READJUSTMENT

Unless they are returning to a difficult home situation, most exchange students are excited and happy when they first return. But they soon learn that their experience is not over yet. They have what is often called reentry shock. Eager to talk to their friends about their year abroad, the students are hurt and disappointed when friends and family show little interest in their experiences. During their year overseas, the exchange students have changed much more than they may realize. They now face the surprising task of learning how to adjust to their own culture again. Some don't experience this problem, but for many, adjusting to the return home is even more difficult than it was to adjust to the foreign culture, because difficulties with adjustment to home are so unexpected.

6

Cross-Cultural Challenges for the Host Family

The exchange program challenges the host families as well as the exchange students. Families are often not prepared for the basic differences in cultural values that they discover when they host an exchange student. Though host families seldom go through culture shock, they do meet with surprising and sometimes upsetting situations as they adjust to having a new and foreign teenager around the house.

Hosting an exchange student is an enormous responsibility. The family must first keep the student safe from harm. This is difficult when exchange students are unaware of dangers they might be facing. "She doesn't understand why we don't want her to walk alone at night," said an American host mother. With the high crime rate in many American cities, parents themselves may be afraid to walk in certain areas after dark. The exchange student seems especially vulnerable to her worried host parents because she does not know the streets nor the precautions she should take.

Host families also act as cultural advisors to the exchange students. They explain the rules of their culture and try to help the student adjust to the society. But host parents are seldom able to think of all the rules they need to teach their guests. As a result, exchange students may embarrass their hosts by their occasionally inappropriate behavior or remarks. For example, in every culture there are some topics which simply cannot be discussed openly. In the United States, it's usually considered rude to ask adults questions concerning their age, their weight, their income, or how much they paid for one of their possessions. Many exchange students don't know these rules until after they have asked such a question.

Other problems may concern the different expectations parents in different cultures have for teenagers. Parents in the U.S. often expect their teenaged sons and daughters to work after school or at least to earn their allowance by doing chores around the house. They want them to be able to find and keep a job, to earn money, and to manage their own finances. In contrast, for example, Portuguese teenagers seldom work while they are living with their parents. If they help out with household chores, they do so in their spare time. Portuguese parents typically give their teenaged children money whenever they need it.

Families can be very settled in their way of life with relatively fixed ideas about how their lives and the lives of their children (including their exchange student) should be lived. The different perspectives the student introduces to the family often cause them to question many of their own opinions, values, and patterns of behavior. Making changes, however, and adapting to the new perspectives is often difficult. Some host families welcome the fresh outlook brought by the exchange student. Others resist any such change and become defensive about their way of life.

The Harringtons were an upper-middle-class family in the northeastern part of the United States. Though they were a very loving family, their behavior was restrained: they seldom hugged or otherwise showed their affection for one another. They had occasional disagreements, but rarely shouted at each other. The atmosphere in the home was calm and peaceful. The Harringtons were quite content with their lives.

Their household changed dramatically when they hosted Iris from Peru. Iris was a lively girl with strong emotions and equally strong opinions. Her family in Peru was affectionate and spontaneous. They frequently hugged each other and, as frequently, shouted at each other. The quarrels were brief, however, and warm feelings characterized her Peruvian family.

The Harringtons had never known someone like Iris. When she hugged them on the day she arrived, they were startled. They hugged her back, though it was awkward for them. Iris was unpredictable. She did not, for example, follow their style of dealing with disagreements. Iris was likely to burst into tears or start shouting in Spanish when she was upset. The Harringtons usually kept their feelings to themselves. They were shocked and a bit frightened by the way Iris carried on. Sometimes they felt they had to be careful so as not to upset her. Gradually, however, they responded to her warmth and enthusiasm. Iris was fun. As time passed, they became less and less worried about upsetting her. They began to see that her dramatic outbursts were momentary and did not change her overall feelings of affection toward them. Their fears about expressing their own emotions began to lessen as well. They found themselves laughing, shouting, and crying more during their year with Iris.

The Smith family's experience was quite different. This midwestern American family believed very strongly in spending time together as a family. Their home was a great source of pride for them. It was always neat. Each family member had specific chores in the house. Most evenings they spent together, talking, watching television, or working on some family project. Their Australian exchange student preferred a more outgoing lifestyle. Kevin enjoyed going out with his friends and felt trapped if he had to spend the entire evening at home. He believed in having fun first and often skipped the chores the family assigned to him. The Smiths did not mind Kevin's desire to go out, nor did they expect him to be as neat as they liked to be. However, Kevin was openly critical of his hosts and complained about their obsession with neatness. He also criticized their preference for staying home. He suggested that this way of life was inferior to the more exciting life he claimed that most Australians led. The Smiths became very defensive in response to Kevin's comments. They began to complain about how poorly Kevin kept his bedroom and started to impose restrictions on his evenings out with his friends to try to force Kevin to stay home more. Though the Smiths might not have wanted to try a different way of living, Kevin's accusing attitude made them hold even more strongly to their own values and behaviors.

In these examples, the attitude of the exchange student affects the family's ability to deal with the cultural differences presented. Though it is not wrong to question or challenge the host family, it is essential to respect their values and beliefs. Changing your host family is not the purpose of being an exchange student. Culture learning is more important. If you can show your respect for their outlook, the host family will be less threatened by the differences between you and more open to learning about your way of life.

Part II

Guidelines and Suggestions for the Exchange Student

Introduction

Having decided to become an exchange student, you have begun the process of learning and growing through an international living experience. At different times in the coming months, your attitudes and feelings will change because of the different stages in your experience. Those described in part II of this book assume a year-long exchange program in which you live with a host family.

But even if you are participating in a shorter program, if you live with a host family, you will still experience many of the same stages. Each of the following nine chapters describes in detail one stage in the experience. The chapters focus on the feelings and situations exchange students like you often experience during particular periods of the year. The diagram portrays each of these stages and its approximate duration.

No one's experience will follow these exact steps. For most students, however, this general pattern provides some insight into the changes they face over the year.

7

Stage 0: Preparing to Go Abroad

FEELING EXCITED, FEELING NERVOUS

Before you leave home, you are at Stage 0, the time of preparation. The exchange organization has sent the news that you have been selected for its program. In the next several weeks, you will receive additional information about your host family and the community in which you will be living for the next year. It is difficult to believe how soon you will be in a new country with a new family. What will it be like?

The eight stages of the exchange experience as portrayed in the diagram below are:

0. Preparation
1. Arrival
2. Settling In
3. Deepening the Relationship
4. Culture Shock
5. The Holidays
6. Culture Learning
7. Predeparture
8. Readjustment

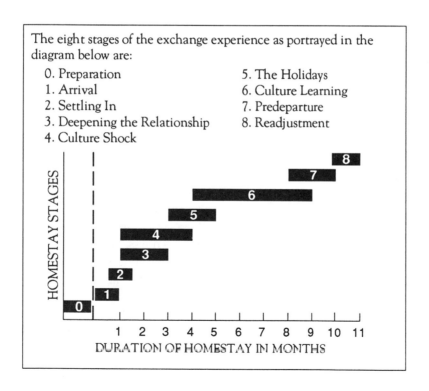

For most exchange students, the preparation stage is an exciting time. You may eagerly search the newspapers and travel magazines for stories about the country you will live in. Each new piece of information only increases your excitement. Yet in the midst of all this excitement, you may also be nervous about the upcoming experience. How will you make friends in this new place? How will you be able to manage in the school while struggling in a foreign language? You may also feel some regret at having to leave your own country. It is normal to have such misgivings. If you are one to worry a little bit about what is ahead of you, that's okay. Perhaps you know your own weaknesses, and in worrying about them you are thinking about how you're going to handle the problems you're anticipating. This can make you better prepared in some ways than students who simply assume everything will be fine. On the other hand, more problems may arise if you are constantly worried about your ability to cope with the exchange experience. Excessive or constant anxiety about travel or about the exchange program doesn't help you prepare for your year abroad.

If you are overly worried, try to manage your anxiety. Think about some of the difficult situations you've faced in the past. How did you cope? How did the situation turn out? Hamida, an Egyptian, remembered how difficult it had been for her when she was put into an advanced math class in her school in Cairo. In the first weeks of the course, she worried a lot about how well she would do. By the end of the year, she had easily passed her exam. Tom, from the United States, remembered the year before and how nervous he had been when he had to make a speech in front of the entire school. He began awkwardly, dropped his notes, his voice sounded strained, and he sweated profusely. A few minutes into the speech, however, he began to relax. He realized he knew his topic well, and his words began to come out smoothly.

Reminding yourself of your ability to succeed in difficult situations can build your confidence. Even if you feel you were not successful, you still survived your difficult experiences and you should be ready to take on the new adventure of being an exchange student. Many of you reading this have already passed a rigorous selection process that included interviews and/or recommendations from your teachers. It is good to remember that these people have confidence in your ability to succeed in the program.

PREPARATIONS

You can't predict all the situations you will meet in the host country. You can't know all the cultural differences you will face or how they will affect your daily life. There are ways to prepare for your exchange year, however, and these preparations will help you get the most out of it.

Reading this book is certainly one step in the right direction. Many exchange programs offer good orientation for the students who are leaving. Their programs and information brochures often include practical advice about packing, visas and passports, and information that will be helpful in an emergency, such as how to contact the exchange organization when overseas. Sometimes former exchange students are available to answer your questions or to lead discussions about what to expect in the coming year. You may also receive information packets that tell you something about family life or school in the host country.

In addition, there are several activities you can do on your own to help you prepare for the year ahead. Here are some of them. You can probably think of others.

Learn the Language. Use any means possible to learn as much of the host-country language as you can before you leave home. Even if you have studied the language in school or in private classes for some time and believe you know it well, the additional study and practice will pay off. There are dozens of strategies for learning a new language, with or without a teacher.[1] All of these strategies require you to use the language. Listening to tapes or radio and video broadcasts in the language is a good place to start if you can. Reading a page or so a day in a language text or other book also helps. If you can find a newspaper from the country you are going to, it is an especially good idea to read it regularly, since you will learn about current issues, problems, events, and interests in the country as well as improve your language skills.

More important is the active use of the language: speaking it and writing it. Unless you are in a class, you will need to create your own opportunities to speak and write. Find people who are native speakers. Practice with others who have studied the language. Write letters or keep a diary in the new language.

Notice what you say to your family and friends and mentally try to put these thoughts in the host-country language. Do the same thing with their responses to you. This rehearsing of your normal conversations will be extremely helpful to you in the host country, especially if your language training has been narrowly focused, on phrases needed by tourists for example, or if your language practice has consisted of translating literature.

Above all, do not be shy or embarrassed by your mistakes (you probably make some mistakes in speaking your own language). You may be surprised at how well others will understand what you are saying despite them. Also, don't get frustrated when you don't know the word you want to use. It may be tempting in such moments simply to switch to your own language to continue the conversation, but you will have missed a chance to learn a new word. Guess at it or ask the person you are conversing with for it. Use the host-country language to describe what you are trying to say. Use words you do know even if they are not exact. For example, a student who does not know the word for post office might ask for the "store where I send letters." At a minimum, use the host-country language to ask for the translation of the word you want.

Study Your Own Culture. Years of experience with exchange programs have shown the importance of students understanding their own cultures. You have probably studied some of the grammar of your language, for example, even though you speak it fluently. Knowing how to recognize a noun or a verb helps prepare you to recognize these parts of speech in another language, even if the rules of grammar are quite different.

In the same way, if you understand some of the rules behind your own culture, you may be better prepared to look for the rules in the foreign culture. This is more difficult than it sounds, especially for those who have never been abroad. Some people compare it to the problem a fish would have in trying to understand water. A fish has never existed without living in water. You have never existed without being immersed in your culture (which includes such things as your values and beliefs, the rules that govern your behavior, and the way you communicate with and relate to other people). Still, there are ways of studying your own culture that can help prepare you for going abroad.

Since many of the rules of a culture are specifically taught to children, you can learn a lot about your culture by noticing what adults teach children. In scolding their children, American parents may tell them, "Look at me when I'm speaking to you." In some cultures, parents will tell their children, "Don't use your left hand. It's unclean." Listen to parents and children and make a note of the things that are considered "rude" or "disgusting" as well as those that are considered "proper" or "polite." If you tried this same exercise in another culture, you would find very different lists of things in each category. By recognizing the rules that you learned, you may be better prepared for different rules in the host culture.

It will also help you to know factual information about your country and its people. When you go abroad as an exchange student, you may be asked questions about your country's system of government or questions about its history, geography, art, literature, or famous places. You will feel more comfortable if you can answer these questions in an intelligent way. In the extreme, you may be called upon to defend or explain the actions of your government.

Write Letters to Your Future Host Family. If the exchange organization has provided the address of your host family a sufficient time before your departure, it is an excellent idea to begin the relationship by writing them a letter. Most exchange students know little about their host families before they arrive on their doorstep. Often they have only the family's name and address. Perhaps they have a picture or some comments written by the family on an application form.

The family does not have much information about you either. Your letter should tell them something about who you are and what you are interested in. Some students like to send pictures of themselves with their natural family and their friends in ordinary situations, working, around home, or having fun. Describe your home and school. Tell them important things about yourself. Use their language, at least for part of the letter. Do not worry about your mistakes. You are unlikely to offend anyone by using the wrong word or grammar. If someone translates your letters or helps you with the language, explain this fact to the host family. Then they will understand that you are not fluent in their language and will not expect you to speak as well as the person who actually wrote the letter for you.

Talk to People from the Host Country. These people can help you learn about the country and can provide useful advice about clothing to take and gifts to pack. People from your country who have lived in your host country will also be able to give you useful information. But be careful. This information may not be objective, especially if the person has strong feelings against or in favor of the country, and it should be compared with information from other sources. The country may have a tourist or trade office in your country where you can get brochures, maps, and other materials at little or no cost.

Prepare for your exchange experience by learning as much as you can before you leave. Remember that the learning does not end at that point. There will be even more to learn when you arrive, and you can use the same techniques there as you did at home.

---

[1]Many of these ideas come from language teachers Joan Rubin and Irene Thompson in their book, *How to be a More Successful Language Learner*, Boston: Heinle & Heinle, 1982. Other helpful books on language learning are H. Douglas Brown's *Breaking the Language Barrier* (1991) and *The Whole World Guide to Language Learning* (1990) by Terry Marshall. Both are available from Intercultural Press.

8

Stage 1: Arrival

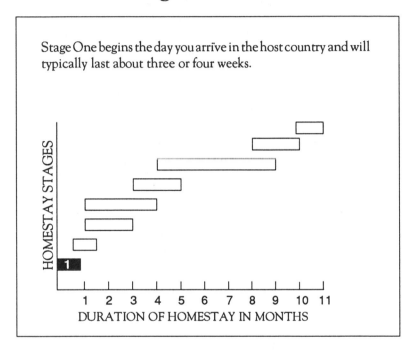

Stage One begins the day you arrive in the host country and will typically last about three or four weeks.

As the plane begins to land, you look out the small window to see this new country. The landscape may surprise you. Perhaps you did not expect the buildings to look like that. Or you did not realize that the country was so dry, or so green, or so mountainous. If this city is not your final destination, keep in mind that many countries have diverse landscapes. Your host community may look very different from the city in which you have just landed. These early impressions can increase your excitement, your curiosity, and sometimes your anxiety as well. As powerful as they are, they don't give you an accurate sense of what it is like to live in this place.

CUSTOMS AND IMMIGRATION

When you cross an international boundary, you must generally pass through government immigration and customs. Some exchange programs have adult leaders who will travel with you and can help you in this process. These leaders must also follow the laws of the host country and cannot change them for you. Though the customs and immigration process is normally simple, it sometimes takes a long time and can be troublesome and confusing. Even frequent travelers become somewhat nervous about customs. You have probably heard stories of people who had trouble with their visa or had a gift they were bringing confiscated by the customs official.

In some countries officials inspect every suitcase. In others, such routine searches are rare. It is helpful to remember that few people have any problems with customs and immigration. When there are problems, they can usually be resolved with relative ease. If you are dressed neatly, have not brought alcohol, plants, food, or large sums of money, and if you are patient and respectful toward the government officials, you are unlikely to have problems.

MEETING YOUR HOSTS

You may recognize them from their photos or they may be holding up a sign with your name on it. Your family has arrived to meet you. What an experience! They are all talking at once. You cannot understand anything they say. They may give you a big hug, or kiss you on both cheeks, or greet you in some other surprising way. Then, suddenly, after everyone has been introduced, it may grow awkwardly quiet, each of you uncertain what to say next.

Don't expect special magic to happen at your first meeting with your hosts. Building a relationship with a family takes time, and you will have plenty of it. The host family may be as nervous as you are. They want you to like them, too. Somehow, the less you worry about the awkwardness of the situation, the less awkward it will be. So relax! Assume that your hosts will like you. Look for traits that you like in them, but be careful not to form opinions about them too quickly. Give yourself time to get to know them.

EXHAUSTION AND JET LAG

If you are not tired when you step off the plane, you can expect to be tired soon. Even if you don't experience a great change in time zones, it is tiring to spend long hours in a plane seat. Too, unless you already speak the same language, you will spend a lot of energy concentrating on what people are saying and how to reply.

Early in your stay, try getting more sleep than you ordinarily need. This is not always possible. Your host family may have planned special events for you, leaving you little time to rest. It is typical for families to want to entertain you as a houseguest during those first days. One exchange student recalled how her family took her with them on a week-long tour two days after she arrived. While she enjoyed herself during this week, she had not adjusted to the time change. The fast pace of the tour made it more difficult for her to recover. Several times she fell asleep in the car and was embarrassed when the family had to wake her to show her sights that she was really much too tired to appreciate.

People who are overtired can get upset by confusing situations and small annoyances that would normally not bother them. Getting enough rest will help you cope better with the unfamiliar and confusing environment.

HEALTH AND CLEANLINESS

Some of the hidden cultural baggage you have brought with you may show itself in the early days of your stay with your host family. Every culture has its own ideas about what is considered clean. In the U.S., a person is clean who showers or bathes daily and uses deodorant. Americans wash their hair frequently—some even daily. They wear fresh underwear each day. Yet most Americans soak in the bathtub in the same water they use to wash themselves. Some Americans see no problem in allowing their dogs to lick scraps from the dinner plates after the meal. In Indonesia an object that is wet is often considered clean. Americans find this upsetting, perhaps because they worry that unhealthy germs and bacteria will grow on wet surfaces.

If your reaction to your host family or their home is, "They are dirty," remember that this is one of the primary red flags that lets you know that differences in culture or values are in operation here.[1] Reputable exchange organizations screen their host families carefully and would not place students in homes they consider dirty. If you watch your hosts, you should discover that their habits include numerous routines for keeping themselves and their surroundings clean. You will probably find ways in which your family is more concerned about cleanliness than you are.

Like many exchange students, you may also worry about your health. It is typical to suffer various minor health problems in the first weeks of your stay in another country. Like other travelers, you may have problems with diarrhea or constipation, which may be a little embarrassing. Or, you might have more trouble than usual with skin diseases such as pimples and acne. Girls may find that their menstrual cycle is abnormal or that they seem to have stopped menstruating. Normally, these problems are temporary and will disappear once your body adjusts. If you are worried about your health, discuss it with your host family. They will be able to recommend appropriate medical care.

FOOD AND DIET

Sharing meals together is an important part of family life. Food is a distinctive and visible part of the culture of a country. Most host families are eager to share their culture by introducing its special foods to their exchange student. You may not like some of the food served to you. Though you want to be polite, don't pretend to like foods that you would not want to eat again. Otherwise you may see them often because your hosts will think you truly like them. Instead, thank the family for giving you the chance to try the new dishes. Save your praise for the foods you really do enjoy.

Similarly, you probably should not refuse out of politeness a dish that you really would like to eat. Students going to the U.S., especially, will find that their American hosts tend to expect them to be truthful rather than merely polite. Chieko, a Japanese exchange student in the U. S., found this out the hard way. In her dreams about coming to the U.S., she always imagined eating and loving American apple pie. On her first night with her host family, she discovered that they had made an apple pie, and she was eager to taste it. However, when they offered her a piece, she politely refused, as is the Japanese custom, not wanting to look greedy. The family assumed Chieko didn't really want the pie and didn't offer it again that night. Americans find this story surprising and amusing, because they expect people to be direct in saying what they want. Remember, you will be there for a long time; formal politeness must eventually give way to the courteous truth.

If the diet you are served by your hosts differs dramatically from what you are used to, there may be other problems. Your own culture's diet depends on certain basic foods and your body has adjusted to using the nutrients from them efficiently. If they are now missing from your diet, you may feel hungry even after you have eaten a large meal. If you come from a culture where rice is a staple at every meal, you may not feel full after eating in the U.S., where rice is not served every day. You might need to eat more food than you normally do. Many exchange students gain weight during their stay in the host country. Don't let this worry you. The added weight is easily lost upon your return home.

RELAX!

Your first weeks in the host country may be hectic, but you will soon settle in as you adjust to the family and community.

---

[1] "Red flags" are discussed in chapter 4. For more information, see Elijah Lovejoy, "red flags," in *Orientation Handbook for Youth Exchange Programs*, Cornelius Grove (Yarmouth, ME: Intercultural Press, 1989), 149-156.

9

Stage 2: Settling In

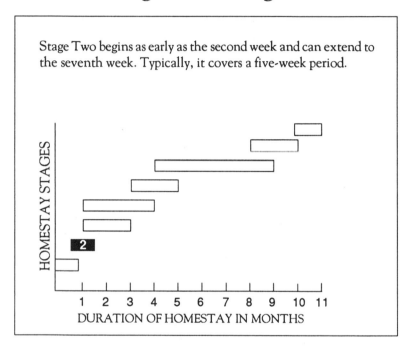

Stage Two begins as early as the second week and can extend to the seventh week. Typically, it covers a five-week period.

After a few weeks in the host family, the initial fatigue of travel should be past. At this point, you're pretty familiar with most of your new family's patterns. In a short time, you have gathered substantial information about them. If you are left alone in their home, you know where to find everything you need. You've developed your own routines that are different from the ones you had at home. The neighborhood should look familiar; you know the major landmarks and how to find your way back home when you go out by yourself. You have begun the process of settling in.

REEXAMINING YOUR GOALS

By now you know a little more about what it means to be an exchange student. You may wonder why you were so worried about it before you left home. The host family likes you, and you like them. You are communicating and feel good about the language skills you are developing. There are differences here, but in many basic ways, it's similar to the way you live back home.

Perhaps you are beginning to make some friends on your own at the school or in the neighborhood and are beginning to explore the community. Or maybe you do *not* feel stouthearted right now, and you are happy to stay close to your hosts and do whatever they do. Each exchange student has a different way of adjusting to the life of the host family and community. Give yourself the time you need to adapt to the new situation, and accept the fact that you may not yet feel fully comfortable.

It may help now to reexamine your goals for the year. Think about the exchange experience as a whole. Write down several features of your stay so far that have been different from what you expected. How do these affect your goals for your exchange year? For example, a Jordanian girl who was visiting the United States was surprised that her host family had a very large dog in the house. Before she came to America, she'd never thought about families having dogs inside their homes. She was afraid of dogs and thought they were repulsive animals. At first, she tried to run away whenever the dog came into the room. But she couldn't keep running, and the family was obviously attached to their dog. This was a difference she had never expected to find. She realized that her fear of the dog was keeping her from spending time with the family. She could see that the family was not going to get rid of the dog, so she would have to change. Her new goal was to try, little by little, to get used to the dog and overcome her fears enough to touch it. Her family gave her advice about how to approach the dog and encouraged her to pet it. Once she was brave enough to touch the dog's head, she began to worry less and less about the dog's presence in the room until finally she was able to ignore it altogether and join in the family life.

You may also discover that your original goals for the program are not realistic. José, a boy from Brazil, had assumed that he and the other young people in his host community would have fun going to dances on the weekends. He could dance well and hoped to have many girlfriends while he was in the United States. After nearly a month in the U.S., he was amazed that there had been no dances yet in the suburban community where he was staying. There were not even any dance clubs or discos that young people in the area could attend. Instead, everyone went to a shopping mall where the boys and girls simply stood around and talked to each other. José knew that his English was not good enough to carry on interesting conversations with girls. He didn't know what to talk about with them, and he often had trouble understanding what they were saying, especially since they used slang expressions much of the time. In reviewing his original goal, José realized that he would not be able to use his dancing ability to get girlfriends. He decided to shift to a new goal: improving his English as quickly as possible so that he could take part in the long, casual conversations that seemed to be the major part of teenage social life in his community. He was fortunate in having a host brother who helped translate the American slang he didn't understand, but he improved even more just by trying to converse. He was delighted to discover that people would listen to him and answer his questions, even though he made mistakes in his English.

FITTING IN

Making friends at school often causes more problems for exchange students than doing well in their studies. It is easy to feel lonely in the first few days when everyone else knows each other so well. Even if the other students are friendly, they may not invite you to have lunch with them or make plans to spend an evening together. You may then wonder what you've done wrong.

You've probably done nothing wrong. In any country, an exchange student must work to make friends. Being an exchange student doesn't automatically make you the most popular student in school. It's not that easy. The exchange program can't simply provide you with a circle of friends the way it's provided you with a host family. Many exchange students have trouble starting conversations with their classmates. They feel shy about suggesting some activity to do together. But why should this be surprising? A new person in any group is likely to feel a little shy. You might worry that the other person has enough friends and isn't looking for more. Or maybe you think the other person won't like you or want to be with you. Most people have felt this way on occasion, but don't let these feelings discourage you from trying to make friends. Too much fear of being rejected could prevent you from making any friends at all.

Where do you fit in? In many schools, most of the students have been with the same group of friends for several years. They may not be looking for new people in their group and may not think of including you in their plans. Others you encounter at school simply may be shy and feel timid about talking to someone from a different country. They may think you wouldn't want to be friends with them. This doesn't make it easy for you.

It takes time to develop friendships, and you may have to be the first one to extend an invitation. Observe the friendship groups in your school or community. Try to discover which people you would like to have as friends. Which people are clearly interested in others? Which ones share your basic values? Which seem to be sensitive to what is going on in other countries? Who is a good listener, and who can be trusted with a confidence?

These are the people most likely to become your friends. The first step is to let them know you want to be friends. In some communities the social life of the young people is governed to some extent by a so-called "popular group" or "in-crowd" whose members attract attention because of their appearance or behavior. You should not be concerned if you have no friends in this group. They may have gained their own status merely by excluding or making fun of others. The existence of such an in-crowd can affect the atmosphere of the school community, but it is most often a very small group. And if you feel excluded by them, many, many others feel excluded too. Outside of that group are plenty of people who will make good and loyal friends.

Sometimes when you get attention from others in the school, it will not be the kind of attention you want. Irene, from Australia, felt miserable in her first month in the U.S. To the American students, her accent was something of a novelty. Some of the girls in her class frequently asked her to repeat phrases that they thought sounded funny in an Australian accent. It seemed to become a classroom joke to speak with an exaggerated Aussie accent. Sometimes Irene would say something quite ordinary, and suddenly the girls would start laughing about the way she spoke. Irene found it hard to talk seriously with any of them and felt they were constantly mocking her. Though everyone knew who she was, she felt that she really had no friends.

Problems of fitting in can also occur within the family. Ahmed, a Turkish boy in the United States, felt excluded by his two host brothers, Jeff and Mike. The brothers had their own pattern of jokes and teasing that did not include him. They often acted very silly together and would toss wild insults back and forth, each one worse than the previous one. It was a competition they seemed to enjoy, so one day Ahmed tried to copy their style and gave his own version of what he thought would be an insult they would appreciate. It didn't work at all. Instead of laughing, Jeff and Mike looked disgusted, making Ahmed feel even more excluded than ever.

Problems such as the ones faced by these two students do not have to be serious obstacles. Ahmed stopped trying to join in the jokes of the host brothers. Instead, he began to talk to them individually. The less he tried to be part of their little two-person group, the easier it was to feel close to both of them. Irene did not need to do anything at all. The girls in her class soon became bored with comments about her accent and began to listen to what she said rather than to how she said it.

If you have trouble fitting in, discuss your feelings honestly with someone from the exchange organization or with a trusted friend or member of your host family. This can often keep a small problem from getting big.

YOUR HOST FAMILY ADJUSTS TO YOU

Since your arrival in their home, your host family has altered their daily routines in a variety of ways to make a place for you. They willingly shifted the time for their showers perhaps. Or maybe they cleared some of their clothes from a closet to let you use it. Even though these shifts are quite minor, they may have caused the family some discomfort. Your hosts may occasionally be annoyed with you over a relatively small matter. You may feel bothered as well when some of the sharing arrangements don't work out perfectly. Maybe you are grouchy because you have to wake up earlier than you would like so that you can have a turn in the bathroom. Living together means having to give as well as take. It also means recognizing that everything will not always work perfectly.

You need to be yourself. You do not have to be just like they are, nor do you have to be the perfect ambassador from your country. You are allowed to have bad moods sometimes, to be unreasonable occasionally, even to do things that may be a little mean or selfish, as long as you pull out of these moods and make a sincere effort to maintain warm and friendly relationships with the family.

ADJUSTING TO SCHOOL

Exchange students often face special problems in adjusting to school. Difficulties with the language may cause teachers to think they should take simpler courses or enroll at a level below their regular academic standing. At other times, the opposite may occur. Some exchange students speak the language well and have a strong academic record from their home countries. When they arrive in the host school, they may be enrolled in advanced classes that might actually be either too difficult or time-consuming. Knowing how much challenge an exchange student needs in the school is difficult to determine in advance. The students themselves often misjudge what they can accomplish in the year.

Secondary schools in the United States frequently offer a wide range of courses and allow students to select many of the classes they take. In other countries, schools are often required to follow a program set by the national government and don't offer the students any choices. Whichever situation you're in, it may be possible to change your course schedule in some way or make special arrangements if there are problems. Your host parents or a representative from the exchange program can sometimes help you explain your situation to the teachers. Present the facts about the problem you are having—for example, you might explain that you need an average of twenty minutes to read a page of moderately difficult text, and the teacher has assigned fifty pages of such reading for the evening's homework. No one expects you to accomplish the impossible. In most cases, special help or an adjustment in the work load can be arranged.

10

Stage 3: Deepening the Relationship

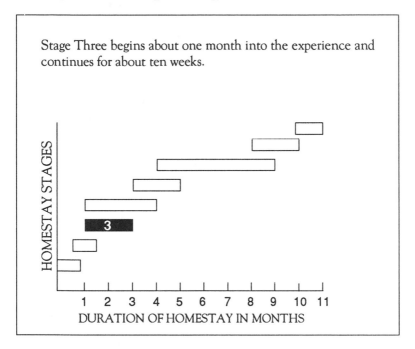

Stage Three begins about one month into the experience and continues for about ten weeks.

HOMESTAY STAGES

3

DURATION OF HOMESTAY IN MONTHS

1 2 3 4 5 6 7 8 9 10 11

RULES, SPOKEN AND UNSPOKEN

All families have rules. In some families, the parents establish the rules very deliberately and will set aside time to teach them to you. This can be disturbing. You may feel uncomfortable or even foolish, and wonder why you can't carry on as you normally do in your own home. Don't they trust you? Do they think you are a small child?

You may not want your hosts to bombard you with all these rules, but this is exactly what your parents should be doing at this stage of your year with them. By being clear about what they expect, your host parents are helping to ease your adjustment to their home and to the community. You need this information, and it is better to hear it now in a discussion with your parents than to find out several months later that you have disappointed them in some way you could have avoided. By including you in the family rules, they are also treating you more like a member of the family and less like a houseguest.

In other families, though, the rules are not very clearly defined. Nevertheless, the exchange student is still expected to follow them. Maybe a month or so into your experience, you may start to discover some of these hidden rules, usually by breaking them first. Some unspoken rules may concern personal topics that are difficult to discuss with anyone not in the immediate family. Though Inga, from Sweden, always dressed appropriately when she went out, her casual dress at home—shorts and a loose T-shirt with no bra underneath—bothered the Mendosas, in Mexico, who felt Inga should dress more modestly with two teenaged sons in the house. But they were uncomfortable bringing up the subject, and they did not want to embarrass or offend her.

Families also may neglect to tell you their rules because they assume that everyone has the same ideas, values, and rules and that you already know them. Every family will be guilty of this at one time or another, which is why it is so important to talk about things like culture and assumptions and values. This will be a problem, because parents in different cultures have very different expectations for good or appropriate behavior in teenagers. Without some research and study, neither you nor your host parents will automatically know where these differences lie.

For instance, Julie, a seventeen-year-old girl from Denmark, was used to entertaining her friends, boys and girls, in her bedroom whenever they visited her home. In Denmark, this was an appropriate place for a teenager to take her friends. Her room is her own space. In her American host family, Julie supposed she would be able to continue this pattern, especially since she had a room of her own. Her American parents, however, assumed that Julie would only bring girls into her room since American teenagers are usually forbidden to bring friends of the opposite sex into their bedrooms. Unfortunately, the first afternoon Julie invited a boy to her bedroom was her last day in her host family. The host parents were furious and informed the exchange program that it would have to take Julie from their home. Julie had no idea what had gone wrong. Though the host parents had never explained their rules, they fully expected Julie to follow them.

The exchange program placed Julie in a new family. On her first afternoon in this family, Julie had a long discussion with her new host mother. She was given time to explain her side of the story and to hear about the rules of this new family. This time, her host mother not only described their rules, but also explained the basis for them. Julie was still expected to follow the rule that no boys were allowed in her bedroom. Now, however, Julie knew the rule and understood the reasons that American parents had for imposing it. Though she did not agree that the rule was necessary, she accepted it and followed it while she was living with her new hosts.

Fortunately, host families seldom react so strongly when an exchange student does something they see as wrong or inappropriate. Still, a student's misunderstandings about family rules and behavior can create bitter feelings on the part of the host family, which frequently lead to other difficulties in the relationship. Julie was unlucky to have hosts who did not explain their rules, but there are ways an exchange student can get information about the family's expectations even when the family does not state them. For one, you can bring up the question of rules and expectations by telling them about some of the rules in your own home or culture. Bill, an American boy in The Netherlands, talked to his host family about the curfew rules his parents set for him back home. Bill explained that in the U.S. he always had to let his parents know where he would be when he went out and that he was always expected home no later than ten o'clock on weeknights and at midnight on weekends. Though his Dutch parents did not actually have any set time for Bill to return home in the evenings, they realized that they had other expectations of him when he went out with his friends. They then began to clarify some of these unspoken expectations. This helped Bill and his host parents understand each other better.

SHARING YOUR CULTURE

Talking about the rules you have back home is one way of sharing your culture with your host family. There are many other aspects of your home culture that you can talk about with your hosts as well. These talks will strengthen your relationship with them and make your stay both more enjoyable and more rewarding. Describing your way of life may help your hosts understand you better and feel more connected to your culture. Some students like to discuss the history or geography of their home country or the political situation there. Others have little interest or knowledge in these areas. You should talk about what interests you most. Talk about the sports you like to play with your friends or the places where you and your friends like to go after school or on weekends. Your hosts will want to learn about your family life. When there are special holidays or festivals in your country, tell your hosts about them and plan to celebrate the occasion together.

Many host families think it a special treat when their exchange student cooks a meal for them that is typical of home. If you like to cook, ask your hosts to suggest a good time to cook something for them. They will probably need to help you a little. Don't be discouraged if you can't find all the ingredients that you use at home or if the pots and pans that your family has aren't right for the dishes you hoped to make. Use what is available and don't worry if it isn't exactly the same as it would be at home. Your family may not like everything you make, but they will appreciate having the chance to try something new.

Your hosts want you to talk about your life back home, but they won't enjoy listening to you describe your country in a way that sounds as if you are claiming it to be superior or your host country inferior. Think about some of these comments made by the host brothers and sisters of exchange students:

> Every time we watch the news on television and see an item about a murder or robbery in the States, Nils has to comment that Sweden has such a low crime rate. I'm tired of hearing this. We have our problems in the U.S., but I'm sure there are problems in Sweden, too.

> Yesterday I had a friend here and we were listening to music and talking. Then Simon came in and started talking about music in Kenya. It seems like he's boasting all the time.

> Susan speaks constantly about her school and her friends back in the U.S. I think she would rather be with those friends than here with us.

Remember that culture sharing means showing interest in your hosts' culture as well as your own. Nils's shock about the crimes described on television is understandable, but instead of constantly comparing the situation in the U.S. with that of Sweden, he could ask questions about the crime problem in the U.S. For example, he might ask what explanations his host family had for the causes for the high rate of crime or if they worried much about becoming victims of a crime. Simon's host brother and his friend might like to hear some Kenyan music if Simon were to show an interest in the music they like. Susan probably feels left out in her host country and really misses her American friends, but by talking only about her friends back home she is excluding those who might now become her friends.

HOST BROTHERS, HOST SISTERS, AND FRIENDS

Susan's difficulty in making friends in the host community is a problem that is common among exchange students. This often affects the student's relationship with the family as well. Host families sometimes consider it a burden to entertain an exchange student who has not been able to make friends outside of the family.

Though the host siblings usually like to include the exchange student in their activities, especially during the first few weeks, no one enjoys being a tour guide forever. Remember, you are not supposed to be a houseguest.

Some exchange students depend heavily on their host brother or sister for everything. They expect to share everything with them and to have a special, intense relationship with them. This is not a realistic hope. Your host sister, for example, may want some time on her own to spend with her boyfriend or her own best friend. You cannot be with her all the time. Your host brother may have a special interest that really does not hold much appeal for you, or vice versa. For example, Uwe's American brother played some sport almost every day. In his home in Switzerland, Uwe's favorite pastime was hiking. Though he tried to join in with his host brother, he was not enthusiastic about sports and really did not want to spend all his time this way. He had to find other friends to share his interests. Like Uwe, you will probably have different interests from your host brother or sister and will also need to find friends who can share these with you.

In many countries, sports and clubs focusing on interests such as photography or computers exist outside of the school. In the United States, they are generally organized within the school framework and meet in the afternoon when classes are over. In these after-school activities exchange students have the chance to meet others in the school who have interests similar to theirs. Many churches and synagogues in the U.S. also have youth-oriented groups and special activities for young people. Your host family may be able to help you find a club that suits you.

Sometimes an exchange student becomes the center of attention in the school from the beginning. Though the attention and popularity this student experiences are often superficial, the fact that the student has become popular in the school can create feelings of jealousy on the part of the host brothers and sisters who feel left out in such cases or deprived of attention they feel they deserve more than the exchange student. They come to resent the exchange student's popularity. If this happens to you, make sure that *you* don't exclude your host brother or sister. If you pay attention to them and include them in your activities, they are less likely to resent you.

When the host brothers and sisters are younger children, they also can become jealous of the attention an exchange student gets within the family. Host parents occasionally sharpen the jealousy by setting the exchange student up as a model of good behavior for the younger children. It is often especially painful for the younger children in the family to hear themselves compared unfavorably with the exchange student. Such comments as, "I wish my own children were as helpful as Greta," or "Why can't you keep your room as neat as Peter does?" can stir resentment that interferes with the relationship between the student and the children and that is difficult to overcome. Even when the children in the family are the same age as the exchange student, the additional attention the parents may give the exchange student can make the brothers and sisters feel jealous. If you sense that your brother or sister is becoming jealous of your position in the family, speak privately to your host parents about your concern. Try also giving more attention to your younger host siblings. This often helps reduce jealousy.

11

Stage 4: Culture Shock

The culture-shock stage begins roughly at the end of the first month and extends until the fourth month. Generally, it covers a three-month period. This stage somewhat overlaps in time with the previous stage.

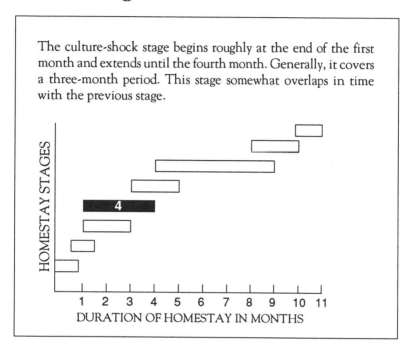

Silvia, an exchange student from Bolivia, liked her American host family, especially her host sister. She had begun to understand English quite well and had few difficulties in her classes. Lately, though, she had begun to feel increasingly uncomfortable. Several days in a row she woke up feeling depressed for no particular reason. Her dreams were more intense than usual and somewhat disturbing. During the day she would burst into tears over minor incidents. She sometimes had difficulty eating. "What is wrong with me?" she wondered.

Silvia was going through culture shock. At first everything was exciting. She felt good about her progress in English. Her new friends were fun and interesting. She enjoyed being an exchange student. She liked her host family and community. What had happened? It was difficult to pinpoint anything in her experience that had really gone wrong. It was, rather, a lot of little things: coping constantly with behaviors that were different and ideas that were difficult to understand, trying to absorb all the new information she was getting, responding in new and different ways to the people around her and to how things were done in this foreign society. Silvia simply did not realize how much effort all this took— and she had to do it in what was to her a foreign language. Silvia, in fact, was exhausted. For this reason, culture shock is often referred to as "culture fatigue."

Silvia was prompted to ask the question, "What's wrong with me?" because she'd always thought of herself as a capable person. She was the kind of person, she had assumed, who would be an excellent exchange student: self-assured, competent, interested in other cultures, someone who got along well with others, always made friends easily, and who could adapt to almost any situation. Clearly the exchange organization that had selected her in Bolivia had also seen her this way. But even while she was adjusting successfully, she began to think that maybe she wasn't the person she thought she was. She discovered that she didn't always feel competent; she could be nervous and afraid sometimes. And she began to doubt herself.

Silvia's confusion about her identity is based primarily on a strongly held image of herself that suddenly didn't seem to hold. Such identity crises are common in this stage of culture shock. The small and large adjustments all exchange students must make to adapt to their new environments may shake their perceptions about who they are. In extreme cases, culture shock can be so intense that an exchange student is unable to continue the experience. Fortunately, this is not the case for most students. Usually, problems of culture shock, or culture fatigue, are temporary. Most students undergo some discomfort and confusion during the early months of their exchange year. Silvia's worry that something was wrong with her probably made her culture shock seem worse. That is why many students are relieved simply to know that their feelings are normal reactions to living in an unfamiliar environment. A former exchange student who has traveled extensively explained, "I feel confused, uncomfortable, and disoriented at times whenever I visit another country. It's a familiar feeling now, so I never worry about it. I try simply to relax and think only about getting through the next hour or the next day. Before long, I'm enjoying myself again."

Culture shock is not a constant depression in most cases. Exchange students going through this stage may frequently feel fine one day and miserable the next. It is difficult to know exactly what will trigger the discomfort and depression. It may be impossible to prevent. There are many ways of coping with culture shock, however, which will help make your life a little easier and will make it easier for your host family as well.

One way is simply to accept as normal a certain amount of confusion or ambiguity. Some students suffer less from symptoms of culture shock because they are more comfortable in confusing and ambiguous situations than others. One Greek girl found it helpful to write in her diary every day. This was something she had done at home when she was upset or confused, and it helped her better understand her thoughts and feelings. As a result, she had few symptoms of culture shock and adjusted quickly to her host community. Other students cope by taking some time alone, by singing or listening to music, or by going on long walks.

Pierre, an exchange student from Paris, was used to walking around the city, visiting the shops, art galleries, and museums. He did this whenever he was feeling anxious or needed to think over a problem. In the suburban American town where he was placed, he could no longer take that kind of walk. No one walked anywhere in his American community, and there weren't any shops or art galleries close to his neighborhood. To get to the nearby city, he needed to ask someone to drive him. At first he had felt excited to be in the United States. A month later Pierre began to find it increasingly difficult to get out of bed in the morning. He often felt sick and was withdrawn much of the time. At this point, the local representative from the exchange organization helped Pierre understand the cause of his problems. She also found someone who enjoyed taking him to the city's art museum and who could introduce him to others who shared his interests.

Part of Pierre's culture shock seemed to be caused by the newly imposed limitations on his independence. He was used to taking care of himself and solving his own problems rather than asking others to help him out. Because he had always been able to find shops and get to museums on his own, he was not really prepared to ask others to drive him. He resented being in the position of having to ask others for favors. When Pierre was able to accept the fact that his dependence was connected with his being in the new culture, he was able to overcome his culture shock. By allowing himself to ask for and receive help, he went on to have a very satisfying exchange experience.

Pierre and Silvia were both faced with situations that confused them. They were frustrated by their inability to cope with the situation and angry at themselves, which left them depressed and anxious. Their recovery from culture shock seemed to follow the stages of anger, mourning, acceptance, and recovery we discussed in an earlier chapter. Silvia wanted to hang on to the image of herself as the model exchange student, and it was painful for her to admit that this image no longer worked. Pierre had to let go of his need to be independent; and since this had always been important to him, he experienced a period of mourning or grief as he tried to deal with a new and unfamiliar situation. Both students were giving up strong, positive images of themselves.

Acceptance is the stage in which Pierre and Silvia were able to live without this part of themselves and to accept the new situation. For Silvia, acceptance meant not needing to try so hard and finding an ability to be just herself and not some superhuman character. For

Pierre, acceptance meant dealing with his need for help without feeling childish in asking for it. Through this process, both students found new skills and new strengths as they began to recover from culture shock.

What can you do if you are depressed or anxious? How can you move from anger to recovery? This list may help.

Avoid Blaming Yourself or Others for the Way you Feel. In *Host Family Survival Kit*, authors Nancy King and Ken Huff compare culture shock to motion sickness. If you felt nauseous and dizzy during a plane flight, you would probably assume that you were suffering from motion sickness. You would not blame yourself for feeling sick, nor would anyone else feel responsible for causing you to feel this way. It is similar to experiencing the symptoms of culture shock. It is not because of any defect in your character that you suffer from culture shock, nor is it the fault of your host family. It is simply a natural result of trying to live in an unfamiliar culture.

Don't Expect Too Much of Yourself. Many students undergoing culture-shock symptoms have difficulty carrying on a normal conversation. They may be unable to pay attention in school and may have trouble simply getting out of bed in the morning. Some students lose their appetites. Others can't stop eating. Setting high, unrealistic goals for yourself will often lead to discouragement. Instead, find ways to reward yourself for small achievements. Try not to take on any additional commitments that would burden your life at this point.

One student who faced this dilemma was Nori, a boy from Japan. Nori was feeling uncomfortable in the U.S. Even in his host family, nothing was as easy as he had expected. Each night he tried to do his homework but could not concentrate on what he was reading. He became frustrated and more and more upset as he realized that he was falling behind the other students in the class. Through an orientation program offered by the exchange organization, Nori learned about culture shock and ways to deal with it. He stopped focusing on how much the American students were accomplishing and began to focus on what he could actually do. He decided to limit his expectations until he could succeed. He might not be able to get through thirty pages of reading in English, but he could maintain his concentration long enough to read and understand two pages. To reward himself for reading two pages, Nori took a break from his homework. He pulled out his pencils and sketch pad to draw for a half hour. Afterwards he was able to return to his reading and eventually could maintain his concentration over a much longer time.

Try to Get More Rest. It is remarkable how helpful it is to take a brief nap of an hour or so, or to go to bed a little earlier each night while you are feeling the effects of culture shock. Students like Nori who are falling behind in their classes may worry that the time lost sleeping will mean even less time available to study. Yet, while Nori was previously spending more time studying, he was getting less done. With adequate rest, your chances of succeeding in your studies are greater. Strain on the emotions is often much more tiring than heavy physical labor, and this will affect not only your ability to learn, but also your ability to cope in general. As mentioned above, culture shock is sometimes more appropriately called culture fatigue.

On the other hand, some students sleep excessively to avoid uncomfortable situations. In such cases, the additional sleep leaves students feeling more tired than before. An hour or half-hour nap before dinner or an extra hour or two of sleep at night is helpful. If you are sleeping more than this and still feeling tired, you should balance the rest with physical activity and face up to the problems that are bothering you rather than avoiding them by sleeping.

Eat Well. Your body also needs proper nourishment to keep going during difficult periods. Whether you have lost your appetite or eat constantly, eat nourishing foods in reasonable quantities and avoid the temptation to eat a lot of junk food such as candy and sweets, soft drinks, and salty snack foods. Even if you do not want to eat anything, try something nourishing at each mealtime. Your physical health is related to how much you suffer from the symptoms of culture shock.

Plan to Do Things You Enjoy. Think about things you like to do, and make plans to do them. Be realistic about the kind of activities you select, but don't give up too quickly if your plans don't work out immediately. For example, if you enjoy playing volleyball or another team sport, you may have to ask dozens of people to find out where you can play or organize a team. It will be worth the effort to find others who enjoy the same activities you do. Even if you don't find a volleyball game, you could find some new friends—with whom you can commiserate about not being able to play volleyball!

Do Not Be Afraid to Seek Counseling or Professional Guidance if Your Symptoms Become Too Intense. Your host family is your first and best source of support in cases of culture shock, but sometimes your problems may involve relations with your host family or may be too difficult or sensitive for you to sort out together. Most reputable exchange organizations have volunteers or staff who are well informed about the symptoms of culture shock. They are ready to provide you with guidance and professional help should you need it. Usually, the sooner you get help the easier it is to deal with the difficulties you are having. If you are on a private exchange or don't know how to contact the exchange organization, you can usually find help through the high school. You might also ask a religious leader such as a priest or minister. It is a good idea to find out how to get help *before* you need it.

Overcoming culture shock is not always easy. Your mind and emotions will work hard to make sense of the strange place in which you now find yourself. The success you have in eventually dealing with a difficult situation will help you be more confident. This is an important step in intercultural learning.

12

Stage 5: The Holidays

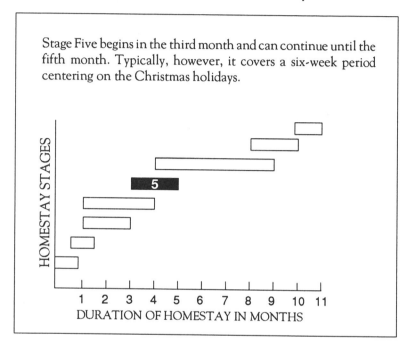

Stage Five begins in the third month and can continue until the fifth month. Typically, however, it covers a six-week period centering on the Christmas holidays.

This stage occurs during the season of the major holidays in the host and home countries and may be experienced differently depending on the customs of the country and where the student is from. For the exchange student in the U.S., this stage typically begins around the end of November and lasts through early January.

After the symptoms of culture shock begin to subside, most exchange students will again feel relaxed in their host families. Yet soon afterwards, many face another shock: the holidays. The holidays described in this chapter are the American Thanksgiving, Christmas, and New Year's celebrations. Exchange students and host families around the world who do not celebrate these holidays may face a similar stage at Carnival, Passover, the end of Ramadan, or the time of any important holiday.

Beginning in late November with Thanksgiving, the holiday season ends after New Year's day. The peak of the U.S. season is Christmas, December 25. Christmas is a Christian holiday, but it is so pervasive in the society that even Jewish families (who celebrate Hanukkah in December) and others who are not Christian find their lives strongly affected by the Christmas season.

The Christmas season is a powerfully sentimental time for families, and a very stressful one as well. Christmas is anticipated as a time of great happiness, when families come together and when people renew old friendships. December is supposed to be filled with parties, food and drink, gift giving, and excitement. Often, though, the actual holiday cannot match the expectations that have been built up for it. If relationships are strained, if there has been a recent death or separation in the family, or if individuals are far away from family or friends, the Christmas season can be painful.

Exchange students in the U.S. are frequently swept up in the festivities of the holidays. And just like their American families and friends, they can also be overwhelmed by the pressures that come with them. But these students frequently face an additional problem that their host brothers and sisters do not. In the holiday season, many families travel to visit relatives and old friends in other parts of the country. A family may welcome four or more people into the home for a week. Or, they may load up the car and drive several hundred miles with their exchange student to stay with relatives a long distance away. In either case, the house is full of new people who are connected to each other in a way that does not include the foreign student.

Mario, an Italian boy, traveled with his American host family in their small car to visit relatives in a distant state. The car was full of luggage, presents, and people, and the interstate highway seemed to stretch on forever. The trip took two days, with an overnight stop in a motel. When they finally arrived, everyone hugged each other and talked about people and situations that everyone (but Mario) remembered. When Mario was introduced, each person asked him how he liked the United States, but there was little else said. He felt no connection to this extended family and just wished he could be back in Italy. On Christmas day, several of the relatives gave Mario presents, but they were still strangers to him, and it was difficult to feel at home.

After the presents were opened and some of the excitement was over, however, Mario found himself telling one of his new "cousins" about Christmas in Italy and the traditions that his family celebrated. As other members of the family joined in the conversation, Mario became more relaxed and began to enjoy himself. His host mother suggested that he call his family in Italy to wish them a happy Christmas. These events helped Mario get through a time of stress and homesickness.

American students abroad may also keenly miss their own families and friends during the holiday season. When students from the U.S. and other countries where Christmas is an important holiday are hosted in countries where Christmas is not celebrated or where its celebration is significantly different or has less importance, they may feel especially let down or depressed. Students sometimes think that Christmas can only be celebrated the way their own families celebrate it. Rather than enjoying whatever activities are going on in the host country, all they can think about is the Christmas they are missing and the friends and families that they are not seeing.

Jennifer, an American girl who lived in Japan for a year, began to feel depressed as Christmas approached. She kept thinking about her parents and brothers and about how they would be decorating the tree and selecting the gifts they would give each other. The Christmas package arriving from her parents made her feel so homesick that she burst into tears. The Japanese are actually quite familiar with Christmas (many Japanese celebrate it) so Jennifer's family and friends understood how she felt. They decided to help her celebrate by bringing her a Christmas cake. Jennifer first thought it was a strange idea to have a Christmas cake. Where was the Christmas tree? Where were the Christmas stockings? What about the Christmas lights and Christmas carols? A cake is for birthdays, not for Christmas, she thought. Still, she knew that her host family and friends were trying to help her celebrate her holiday. As she thought more about their kindness and concern for her, she realized that her Japanese Christmas was also going to be a special time.

If you feel lonely or depressed during the holiday season, there are several steps you can take to maintain a more positive outlook.

1. Remind yourself that no holiday can live up to the expectations of the kind that are raised by all major holidays like Christmas. Try not to concern yourself with what the holidays are supposed to be or how much you are supposed to enjoy them. You have not failed as an exchange student if your Christmas, Diwali, New Year's, Carnival, or other traditional holiday season is not perfect. Remember, over the years there will be many more to meet your expectations.

2. Find some way to share an aspect of your holiday celebration with your host family. Prepare some special holiday food and tell them a story about the holiday in your country. You might want, for instance, to give them presents from your home country associated with the holiday.

3. Focus on the activities taking place here and now and not on whatever it is you might be missing back home. If you worry too much about events and people you miss, you will also miss out on what is happening in your host country. Your exchange program year includes spending the holidays in your host country, so plan to take part in that experience, whatever it is.

13

Stage 6: Culture Learning

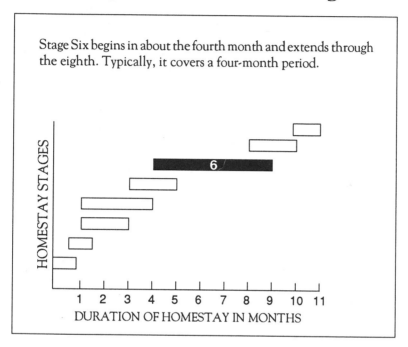

Stage Six begins in about the fourth month and extends through the eighth. Typically, it covers a four-month period.

The culture-learning stage normally occurs about halfway through the experience. For some students it may come much later. For a few, their major culture learning occurs after they return home.

WHAT YOU HAVE LEARNED

By now you have probably begun to notice how much progress you have made in understanding this new country and culture, especially the language. If you already had a good foundation when you arrived, you can probably carry on a complex conversation with almost anyone. Even if your linguistic skills were weak before you came, by now you can understand most conversations and can make yourself understood as well.

You may be surprised to realize how much you have changed in just a few months. Do you remember what you were like when you first arrived and what those first impressions of your host country were? Most of your early impressions have been long tossed aside as you've become used to the new ways and understand more fully the culture in which you now find yourself. Looking back at her first impression of the American girls in her school, Ulla from Finland remembered:

> They wore so much makeup! The girls here seemed shallow and materialistic to me then. They talked only about clothes and hairstyles, boys, and rock music. And they were hardly concerned with any of the real problems of the world. But now I see them much differently, and I understand better their concerns and the way they live. I don't even notice their makeup anymore; it seems fairly normal to me now.

When Ulla got to know some of the girls in her class better, she discovered they had much deeper interests and commitments seldom mentioned in casual conversations after school. When she spent time alone with individual classmates, she discovered that Christine was involved in political causes, edited the school's literary magazine, and wrote poetry and book reviews. Dawn spent hours every day training in ballet and taught dance to a class of younger children. Sandy, who became one of her best friends, spent her Saturdays working at a senior center, helping with the lunch program. Ulla began to question her own ideas about what the real problems of the world were and what girls her age should talk about with each other. For example, after going with Sandy one day to the senior center Ulla found herself thinking more and more about her own attitudes toward the elderly and how different societies take care of their old people. She was struck by Sandy's commitment to the senior center and commented: "I came to understand that the real problems of the world include the fact that there are people too old and weak to feed themselves."

More than this, Ulla found out that she could also let herself be a little less serious in her conversations and have some fun. The time she spent hanging out with the others after school gave her a chance to relax and enjoy herself before going home to study.

Culture learning is more than the obvious improvement in your language skills and the fuller impression you have formed of your surroundings. Like Ulla, your learning at this stage takes place on a much deeper, more personal level. As you begin to question the way you view the world and experience new ways to deal with life situations, you learn about yourself. As you grow comfortable and confident in the new culture, you become more aware of the culture you have brought with you and more open to examining your opinions and ideas objectively. In doing this, you begin to discover new attitudes and values within yourself. Ulla had often talked about politics and world affairs, but she now saw that this was only talk and that she had not actually done anything specific to make a difference in the world. Now she had a new perspective. Her idealism grew stronger, and she felt a greater need to get directly and personally involved instead of merely talking about it.

Like Ulla, you may have gained some new insight into yourself, your ideals, and about people in this new country. Research on educational exchange indicates that there are several distinct areas of learning and personal growth that appear to be related to the experience. The greatest learning, of course, occurs in the increase in knowledge about and awareness of the host country, its culture, and its language. But exchange students also learn about their own culture and about culture in general and become more aware of the complexities of international issues than those who stay home.

As an exchange student, you are learning by doing, not by sitting in a classroom or studying books. It is what you learn outside the classroom that is most important. Learning by doing means that what you learn stays with you longer. How many times have you studied a book or class notes just to pass an exam and afterwards quickly forgot whatever you'd learned? This happens frequently when you don't use the new information. But as an exchange student, you need the new information to handle your everyday life, your work at school, and even your fun. For this reason, it sinks in deeper, and your memory of it is much stronger.

When you learn something well, when you succeed in understanding new ideas, when you can easily carry on a conversation in another language, you also gain a strong sense of self-confidence. This helps you worry less about making mistakes. If you are not anxious about your mistakes, you are willing to reach out further, try new things, make new friends, and learn even more.

FRIENDS ARE IMPORTANT

Friendships are crucial to culture learning, because your friends will introduce you to new ideas and outlooks that you could never discover on your own. When you become friends with others, you start to understand who they are. Through your empathy with them, you learn about their outlooks on the world and what it is like to be *them*. You can learn from their experiences as well as from your own. This is something that Ulla found out through her friendship with Sandy. How well you adjust to the new culture and how much you learn are directly related to your ability to form and maintain friendships with people from your host country.

You may become very good friends with other exchange students living nearby. Since you are all going through the same experience, you may want to be in close contact with them. These friends may be among your most cherished, though if you only make friends with other exchange students, you miss a special part of the experience of being in this culture and some of the most intense and significant culture learning.

There are other kinds of learning and growth which are typical during the year abroad. Students become more adaptable and more critical and independent in their thinking. They are better able to assume responsibility for themselves. They can communicate better with others. Exchange students also develop a stronger sense of their ideals—they tend to be less materialistic. They come to appreciate better their own countries and cultures.

This learning won't stop now. You will continue to learn how to look at the world differently, how to communicate better, and how to think more clearly. You will understand better who you are and the cultures that have shaped your values and ideals. For most exchange students, culture learning continues throughout their lives.

FEELING AT HOME WITH THE FAMILY

The early concerns that you had about making a good impression are gone by now. The host-family home and community are familiar and comfortable. Most of the time you know what to expect. Your life probably has begun to feel ordinary. You can even get bored. It's no longer all new and different.

In the culture-learning stage of the experience, the exchange student is living a normal life with the host family. The sense of comfort and even freedom occurring at this stage does not mean that everyone gets along perfectly. Does any family get along perfectly?

The very fact that the family and exchange student feel more comfortable with each other introduces the possibility of new sorts of cross-cultural misunderstandings. They have begun to behave as they do with family and close friends and are less polite with one another. Being close does not eliminate occasional hurt feelings and bewilderment as the host family and the exchange student continue to behave in ways that are sometimes incomprehensible to each other. New assumptions can emerge that show up new and unexpected cultural differences. Families and students who have been open with each other and who dealt with small misunderstandings in the early days will be able to cope with new misunderstandings and use them as opportunities to discover more about themselves and the cultures they come from.

Jessica, the only child in her American family, liked having a new Argentine brother, Miguel. Through the year she and Miguel had many heart-to-heart talks and had become quite close. He felt like a real brother to her. Frequently she confided in him about problems she had with her boyfriend or misunderstandings she had with her mother. She teased him about the girls he liked at school. To Jessica, Miguel seemed more mature than the American boys his age, less silly and more of a gentleman. He was someone she felt she could trust.

Her impression of Miguel changed dramatically when one of his Argentine friends came for a visit. She was shocked as she heard the two boys discuss a criminal case concerning a man who had killed his wife when he discovered she had taken a lover. The boys were sympathetic with the husband and seemed to feel that the wife "had it coming to her." They began to make jokes about the situation, which Jessica found extremely offensive. Jessica said nothing at first, but Miguel sensed immediately that she was upset. Later he talked to her about it, though he was not really sure what aspect of the conversation had made her upset. But the more he tried to explain himself, the more he seemed to upset Jessica. She sympathized with the murdered woman and accused Miguel of using a double standard that allowed men to ignore their marriage vows while if women did the same, they were killed for it.

Both Miguel and Jessica spent the next few days thinking a lot about the roles of men and women. When they tried to talk about it, Jessica often was reduced to tears and Miguel became moody. But they did keep talking, and both of them gradually found ways to bridge the gap that had developed between them. Miguel began to understand a little better why Jessica with her high moral values might still sympathize with a "bad" woman. Jessica eventually concluded that she expected too much from Miguel, since his experience was different from hers. Instead of arguing with him, she began to talk to him more about what it was like to be a young woman in the United States and how she felt when she heard the story about the woman who was killed by her husband. Miguel told her about his own upbringing in Argentina and how his parents played very different roles in the family and society.

No matter how close you have become to your family, some of your attitudes or reactions to daily events could still offend your hosts in some way you can't foresee. If you are able to discuss your differences in outlook and behavior and really listen to each other, your relationship will be stronger, and these misunderstandings can become great opportunities for learning and personal growth.

Learning how to live with differences is part of the set of skills you are developing as an exchange student. Showing respect for others, listening to them, and being genuinely interested are critical in building close relationships—especially across cultures.

OTHER CHALLENGES

Intense Emotions. One area of culture learning that is often difficult for exchange students and their hosts concerns the way in which people express intense feelings. You may recall the case of Iris from Peru and the Harrington family described in chapter 6. In many cultures, expressing feelings is an important part of personal relationships. People in these cultures describe themselves as warm, genuine, or passionate. Iris would describe herself that way. Those from other cultures may view them instead as hot-tempered or unpredictable, which is how the Harringtons tended to view their Peruvian daughter in the first months. In such cultures, expressions of strong emotions are seen as a threat to the harmony between people; Iris frightened her host family when she lost her temper. For them, emotional outbursts suggested a lack of control and maturity, while they would see themselves as calm and reasonable. On the other hand, those coming from the more expressive cultures might view people like the Harringtons as cold and unfeeling.

For the exchange student (and the host family) this is one of the major challenges of culture learning: to deal with new and intense feelings that occur in unfamiliar settings and uncomfortable ways. Culture learning is not a matter of shutting off these feelings, but of using them to learn and grow. By becoming more aware of the different values and choices that are possible in human society, you gain a better appreciation of your own society and culture.

Cabin Fever and Boredom. Toward the end of the winter months, especially in colder climates, many exchange students feel isolated from the outside community. When the weather is cold or wet for a long time, the members of the household are more or less forced to remain indoors with only each other for company. The resulting frustration and boredom, coupled with having to endure the annoying habits of other people, is known as cabin fever.

If the winter is not severe, or if good public transportation exists, the exchange student may avoid this problem entirely. In many locations in the U.S., Canada, and other countries in extreme northern latitudes, the winter is very cold, and the only way to get anywhere is to shovel snow first, then warm up the car—and find someone to drive you where you want to go. The feeling of being trapped in the house can be strong and difficult to endure as the winter drags on.

The only solution at times is to make the special effort required to get out of doors. Take advantage of winter sports and other activities. The cold or rainy weather does not have to prevent you from having fun. It is also useful to find new ways of passing time indoors. After checking with your family, invite friends from school to come over. New people in the house bring a new level of energy and interest.

The cold weather will eventually change, ending cabin fever. But by then you are probably coming close to the end of your year abroad.

14

Stage 7: Predeparture

Stage Seven begins near the end of the homestay experience, approximately six weeks prior to your departure, and ends when you actually return home.

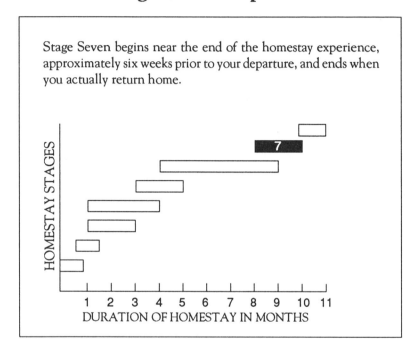

You always knew you would be going home at the end of the year but suddenly the time is upon you. The exchange organization has written you about your return flight arrangements. Your family back home has written you about plans they are making for your return. Soon you will see your own family and old friends again. You will be able to enjoy some favorite foods you have missed all these months. Yet even while you're feeling excited about your return, there is something spoiling it.

You don't want to leave! You have made good friends here, friends who have helped you through some difficult periods and shared some of the best times you can remember. You have a host family that you have come to love. You have started a new life that you are really enjoying. Maybe you have just found romance with a special person. You find yourself asking, "Why do I have to leave? Why now?"

Mixed feelings are normal in this situation. You miss your family and friends back home, but feel uneasy about rejoining them. You've changed in many ways this year. Though you have written to them often about all that you've been doing, your family has not been with you to see these changes. You have shared this past year with your host family, and it hurts to leave them. Will your own family understand? This confusion can leave you exhausted, but there is no time to rest. You still have so much left to do and so many people to see before your departure. Maybe you have had some troubles over the year and want to set things straight before you leave. This added pressure certainly does not make it easier for you.

It may be tempting to pretend that departure is still a long way off. Some exchange students refuse to pack boxes to ship back home, or they misplace their passports or airline tickets. Ignoring reality does not change the facts. Students who avoid thinking about leaving and about packing find themselves rushing furiously in the last two days. In such an atmosphere, the only conversation possible is about schedules, passports, tickets, and luggage. There is simply no time to share important feelings. As Joyce, an American girl, recalled:

> That last day with my host family in France was pretty hectic for me. I know I was being difficult. I had to buy gifts for everyone back home. There was too little time. I hadn't even checked my ticket or reconfirmed my flight. We were bickering all day, and when they left me at the airport I could only cry. There was so much I should have told them, but that day it was impossible.

Thoughts of departure can often make everyone feel angry and depressed. Just when you have finally adjusted, are feeling at home in the new culture and family, and can speak the language well enough to have really good conversations, it ends. As one exchange student said, "Now that I'm no longer homesick, I have to go home. It isn't fair." Students and their host families who have overcome serious problems during the year may particularly resent the upcoming departure because after all the effort to work things out, there is too little time left. This was true with Ellen, an American host sister whose frequent fights with Juan, her Mexican brother, had caused major difficulties for everyone. By the end of the year, Ellen and Juan were finally on good terms. There had been so much time wasted in conflict that she felt cheated that he was going to leave now. "Earlier in the year I wanted him to leave, but now I know him better. Now we are getting along and having fun. It upsets me that now he has to return," she complained.

The sadness of the approaching departure was particularly strong for Barry, a New Zealander, who had become part of a close circle of friends during his stay in the United States:

> When you've got a group like ours, you want it to last forever. Toward the end of my stay I began to realize that this was the last time for so many things. I was returning to New Zealand; at the end of the summer they would be leaving too—each to a different university. Our group was scattering and I got pretty depressed because I knew there would be no way for us to get back together again.

Any great change in life involves losing as well as gaining something. It is natural to be upset and depressed about the part that is lost. You can't prevent having these feelings, but you can prepare yourself for them and prevent them from interfering with your relationships with the host family and friends. There are several steps you can take to help you cope successfully in this stage of your experience:

Recognize Feelings. As the end of the year approaches, you need more than ever to examine your thoughts and reactions and understand your feelings. You, like most students, will probably have a number of different and maybe conflicting emotions as you prepare to leave. You may be nervous, relieved, sad, angry, and confused. All these feelings will affect your behavior to some degree. By recognizing them and how they affect you, you can begin to soften that impact.

Accept Feelings of Loss. It hurts to leave family and friends and to know that the good times together will soon come to an end. In going home you are completing an important stage of your life. While you may have developed close relationships with your host family and others that will continue to be important to you for years to come, you will never share your life with these people in quite the same way again. Some exchange students are afraid to face the sadness of leaving and try to push away their thoughts about missing their new families and friends. This does not work well. The loss is real, and the hurt does not go away by ignoring your feelings about it. Accepting and understanding your feelings of loss will allow you to overcome some of your fears about returning. Remember also that your host family and friends are going to miss you when you leave. Sharing the feeling of loss may make it easier for all of you.

Prepare for the Separation. Some students find it difficult to separate from their host families because they are afraid of hurting their hosts' feelings by appearing too eager to return home. One girl recalled:

> On the day I left, I became very excited about returning home and seeing my parents again. My suitcases were packed and I was ready to go. My host father surprised me by asking if I was sad about leaving the United States. I wasn't really sad then, but what could I say? I was afraid he would think I didn't like them or the States.

You and your host family need to prepare for your departure long before the last day. One way to do that is to share with your family some of your hopes and plans. Tell them what you will be doing with your family and friends when you get back. Tell them also what you'll miss from your life with them. And show them. For example, you might ask for the recipes for some of the foods you have especially liked. Let them know how much you'll miss the time you spent together. This can be done in many different ways. Some students select special gifts that relate to those times together. An Austrian girl who spent each afternoon after school chatting with her host mother over a cup of coffee decided to buy two matching coffee mugs, one for herself and one to give to the mother. Another student bought matching T-shirts for himself and his three best friends. These kinds of gestures help bring to a close this part of your relationship, while signaling to your host family and friends that you will not forget them and your experiences together.

Review the Experience. In this day of rapid international travel, it will only be a matter of hours from the time you step on the plane until the time you are back home. When you return home, you should be ready to focus your attention on your life there. It helps if you have taken the time before your return to review your year as an exchange student, because this allows you to complete the year and leave it behind. Like other major events in your life, the end of your year as an exchange student should be commemorated in a meaningful way. Spend some time with your host family and friends talking about your first days here and the various experiences you have had together. Talk about the way you felt when you first arrived. Remind them of the funny things you may have done when you didn't fully understand the culture. Think of some of the highlights of your year and some of the more difficult times as well. Discuss how much you have changed since then and how much you have learned.

By reviewing your entire experience, you are less likely to become obsessed with small regrets about things you wanted to do or things you wish you'd done differently. Your year has been one of learning, of building friendships, of discovering a new place, and of getting to know more about yourself. In all this you have succeeded, as one of the most significant years in your life comes to a close.

Prepare for Reverse Culture Shock. This is also the time to prepare for reverse culture shock. When you arrived overseas, you knew some things would be different and that you would have to adjust. Now that you're going home you may not think that culture shock will be a problem for you. You're in for a surprise! For many exchange students, coming home is even more difficult than going abroad. Part of the reason for this is precisely because no one expects to have problems going home, and so students return home unprepared to cope with them.

You may be able to prepare by reminding yourself that, during this year, changes have occurred both in yourself and at home. You cannot simply return as if this year had not happened. It may be helpful to think of times in the past when you returned to a familiar place and found that it changed. Maybe your attitudes about it changed as well. Maybe this was a place you loved to visit when you were a small child, or a school you formerly attended, or the neighborhood where you once lived. Remembering your feelings on these occasions may help you recognize them again when you return home.

Clare, for example, remembered very clearly the time she revisited her nursery school ten years later. "I used to think the classroom was so big," she remarked. "Now it looked small to me." Some of the books Clare remembered were still there, and she could remember how much she loved sitting on the rug and hearing the stories. The playground equipment was the same, too, but seemed much smaller. Her sadness at realizing she didn't belong now in this school that she had once loved was mixed with the pleasure of watching the younger children working at the small tables or sitting on the rug to hear a story.

As Clare thought about going home, after a year abroad, she remembered this old experience of visiting her nursery school. Would her home seem smaller or different to her now? Would she feel much older? Would she feel sad about what she found back home? How would it be different and how would she be different? Clare had only visited her nursery school; now she would be returning home to stay and would have to adjust to whatever changes she found in her home and in herself.

You may be worried about some aspect of your return. Perhaps you are facing school exams or academic problems caused by missing a year of school back home. Maybe you are concerned that your family and friends will not be interested in hearing about your experience. Maybe you realize how much you've changed and think that you will not fit in with your group and the life at home. Things may have changed at home too. Your little brother may now be taller than you. Your sister may have taken over your favorite chair or your bedroom. Your parents may have settled into a new pattern of doing things while you were gone. Cynthia's mother had started working and was no longer home all afternoon. Though her mother had written her about the job, Cynthia had not realized that dinner at home was now eaten much later and frequently came straight from the supermarket freezer.

While you cannot deal with these changes before you return, it is useful to think about them and to discuss them with your host family. It may be helpful to remember that many, many others have dealt with similar problems. You have gained some valuable skills in adjustment as a result of your experience as an exchange student. Keep a positive attitude about yourself and your own abilities.

Plan Your Farewell. Actually saying good-bye is never an easy task, but it is a very important one. In his journal just before leaving London to return to the United States, Victor Hunter wrote:

> Today I must say good-bye. Good-byes are important. Without a meaningful good-bye, an effective closure, there cannot be a creative hello, a new beginning and hopeful commencement. I have always found it important to mark the times and the seasons, the significant events in my life and my family's life, with ritual and symbol.[1]

It would be a shame to leave at the end of a year without marking the occasion in some special way. Don't wait until the last day to think about how you want to say good-bye. Students I have known have written special letters or poems or made an audiotape to leave with members of their host family. Others may make a speech or a toast at a special farewell dinner or party. Some give symbolic gifts such as the coffee mugs and T-shirts mentioned before. Probably most exchange students take a final photograph together with their host family. How do you want to say good-bye? Planning your farewell is an important step in your journey home. It probably will not happen just the way you plan, but it doesn't have to be perfect to be meaningful to you and your family.

Good-byes are especially important for romantic relationships. Much of what has been discussed in this chapter also applies to serious romances. If you had a special boyfriend or girlfriend, your last days together are likely to be highly emotional and tense. You may be desperately trying to find some way to be reunited soon. Romantic relationships do sometimes survive a lengthy separation, but obviously there are many obstacles in your way. While you may always love each other, your departure will definitely change your relationship. So even if you hope to continue an international romance, you must accept that the present phase of your relationship is coming to an end. Talk together about the special times you have had; these memories will be important to you when you return. Make plans to write to each other. Your future together is necessarily uncertain; it may be a long time before you see each other again. By then your circumstances and your relationship will have changed. In spite of the pain of separation and the uncertainty about the future, you may always feel fortunate to have had this romance to remember and treasure.

Now you have finished the year. All your packing is done. You've said your good-byes. You are ready to give those final hugs, shed those final tears, and step on the plane. Yet your experience is not over, as the next chapter will show.

---

[1] Victor L. Hunter, "Closure and Commencement: The Stress of Finding Home," in Clyde N. Austin, ed., *Cross-Cultural Re-Entry: A Book of Readings* (Abilene, TX: Abilene Christian University Press, 1986), 179.

15

Stage 8: Readjustment

Stage Eight begins with the exchange student's departure and usually continues for three to six weeks, though it may continue for several months.

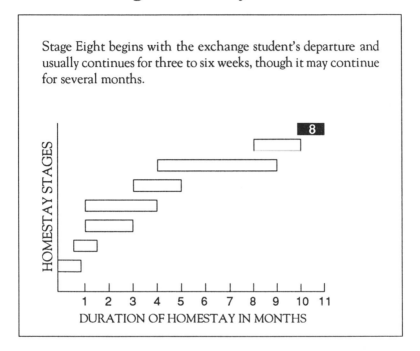

Your exchange program does not really end when you return home. In fact, many exchange students are surprised at the difficulty they experience in coming home. For the returned student, the process of learning about "home" is often similar to the process of learning during the stay in the host country. There is once again an adjustment cycle.

Stage 1. Excitement, relief, confusion, and surprise all come together as you meet your family and friends, speak your own language again, and use your own country's currency once more. You return quickly to some of your old patterns of behavior, except now they feel strange. You are surprisingly awkward in your movements, too conscious of them. Lakshmi had worn jeans and skirts in the U.S., but back in India, she wore saris again. She had not forgotten how to make the pleats in the front and wrap the six meters of fabric around her. These motions came automatically. The first several days, though, she stared at her hands as she worked the pleats. Before she went to the U.S., she took these actions for granted. Now she experienced them as "foreign," and it seemed to her as if she were dressed in an Indian costume, rather than wearing her own clothes. Even her language was different; when she spoke English, people commented on her American accent and patterns of speech, and when she tried to speak her own language, it sounded strange in her ears. Like Lakshmi and many other students, your own language may not come easily at first.

You will also soon discover that a few changes have occurred in your absence. Perhaps there's nothing major that's new. Maybe your mother is wearing a dress you never saw before. There may be some new piece of furniture in your home. Perhaps your parents have painted their bedroom a different color. You may have new neighbors in the building next door. Your cousin might have a new girlfriend. These sorts of changes are not really important, but they are unexpected. You weren't around to see them happen. Somehow you had expected time to stop while you were away. You may feel a little uneasy realizing that your family, friends, and the community in which you live did not stay exactly the same while you were gone.

Stage 2. Though you soon settle back into the familiar routines, new difficulties begin to surface. Returning students are challenged in at least two areas of their lives in their home countries.

The first occurs in the realm of education and career. Like many exchange students, you may have returned from your year abroad with new ideas about what you want to study or what type of career you want to pursue. In some cases, you may have difficulty changing plans you set in motion before you went abroad. In school you can have other difficulties. You may have missed important deadlines or examinations required for university entrance. You may not be able to receive academic credit for your schoolwork in the host country.

To further complicate matters, you could face a changed national economic or political environment. Such changes often interfere with a student's educational or career plans. University strikes or difficult economic conditions may make it seem impossible for you to attain your goal of going to college for advanced study or getting a good job.

Even if you've finished secondary school and have little trouble enrolling in a university program or if your secondary school recognizes your work abroad and lets you move ahead with your former class, you may still have trouble readjusting to the classroom culture and the demands made by the university or secondary school in your own culture. Instead of concentrating on your studies and the work at hand, your thoughts tend to turn to your recent experiences as an exchange student. Perhaps you think that the school system in the host country seems better than the one at home. It may have been more relaxed, or more challenging, or simply more interesting than the classroom in which you now sit.

The second type of challenge returning students face involves relationships with family and friends. Like many students, you may feel you have matured faster than your friends who did not go abroad. Conversations with them seem shallow and less interesting than you remembered. There is frustration too. Friends back home are seldom as interested in your experiences abroad as you are eager to talk about them. You have been through profound changes, but their importance is not recognized by those who were once close to you. Instead, they quickly switch the conversation to another topic.

Even your parents, though they usually will listen to you and are interested in what you have to say, don't seem to understand how much you have changed or how important this year has been to you. They may reimpose old childish restrictions on you. Worse, they may recognize that you have changed and try to make you change back!

Stage 3. The real challenges of readjustment begin to surface at this point. Unable to slip into your old place in your society or in your family, you struggle to find a new niche for yourself. You may have an identity crisis, feeling detached not only from the culture you have just left but from the home culture to which you have just returned. It is typical for exchange students to develop a sense of both isolation and superiority. You feel isolated because your old friends don't understand you and superior because you feel more mature, sophisticated, and knowledgeable about the world than they.

On the other hand, you may have a strong need to belong to your old circle of friends. You may try pretending that you haven't really changed very much and hope you will eventually return to your old self, the way you were before you left home.

Stage 4. Eventually you will find ways to reconcile the differences between the two cultures and readapt to the life of your own society. You may relieve your sense of isolation by seeking other exchange students or people from different cultures as friends. You develop a deeper appreciation of how you have changed and how much you have learned, and this is valuable in itself, apart from your relationships at home or school.

The challenges you face as you try to get interested in your life here, resume your studies, or find employment are all part of the normal adjustment and learning process. You have returned home with new ideas, a new outlook, and new skills gained in the host country, and obviously you don't want to discard these new aspects of yourself just to fit in again back home. After the initial readjustment to the way of life at home, you may be homesick for your other home abroad. How can you bring the culture home with you?

Exchange students often find creative ways of meshing the best aspects of both cultures. For example, Arlene discovered that she could bring a little of Chile to the United States by being more openly affectionate with her family and friends. Though she had seldom hugged her American parents since she was a teenager, now she gave them big hugs all the time. They seemed to like this change as much as she did.

No matter where you live in the world there are many ways to connect with foreign countries. You may not have been aware of them before your year abroad, but they are there and will now enable you to continue some of the activities you enjoyed in your host country. Uli found a sports club in Germany where he could play American baseball. Marcia found a class in Japanese calligraphy. Tim started watching the Spanish television station and found some of the same programs he had watched in Venezuela.

There are also other, more significant opportunities which your year abroad can provide and which you can fit into your life at home. Max, who spent a year in Malaysia, came home deeply impressed by the need to preserve one's own culture in the face of modernization. Since he was American, not Malaysian, he focused on his own culture and threw himself into studies of early American history, literature, and folk crafts. He decided to become a museum curator with a mission to educate Americans about their own culture.

Hélène's year in the United States brought her into contact for the first time with African Americans and made her aware of some of the problems of racism. Back in France, she was now more aware of the problems of racism in her own society. She began reading about the issues facing immigrants to France and the nationalist movement that opposes immigration. Though she had clearly seen that the U.S. was no shining example of racial harmony, she was drawn to the ideals of a society made up of immigrants where, at least in theory, everyone belonged. Hélène joined the group SOS Racisme and began to work to put these ideals into practice in France.

The readjustment cycle is sometimes long and demanding. Exchange organizations can help by providing special programs and social events to bring together former exchange students. Many returned students find it helpful to work with foreign exchange students in their countries or with those planning to go abroad on the next cycle. Keeping in touch with host family and friends also helps ease the sense of loss. When possible, a return visit later on can sometimes help former exchange students resolve remaining contradictions and questions.

Returning home is the final stage in the culture-learning process, but the learning continues long after the readjustment. The new perspective gained from the year abroad continues to be broadened.

Because exchange students have once opened their minds to the host culture, their minds can remain open to other cultures and new ideas. For this reason, years after they return home, many people report that their year abroad as an exchange student was one of the most significant events of their lives.

Postscript
Special Issues and Concerns

Though this book has outlined the stages of an exchange student's experience, it is not possible to predict everything that will happen at each stage of the sojourn. There are also special circumstances that may dramatically change the type of experience a student has in the host country. Two of these special cases are actually quite common.

1. Changing Host Families

One of the most difficult experiences an exchange student may encounter is the need to change host families. Despite careful efforts to find the right family for each student, it is inevitable some will have such unsatisfactory relations with their initial family that they will have to be moved. Some organizations report that roughly one in four students on year-long programs changes host families. While both the students and the families may have made some mistakes, it is usually no one's fault if the placement does not work out. Exchange organizations typically make placements on the basis of application papers. Pieces of paper can never represent the real person, nor can anyone accurately predict how a given student and family will react to each other.

If you are having a difficult time adjusting to your host family, seek help. Most reputable exchange programs have representatives available to advise students who are having trouble. Frequently, an outside person with experience in exchange programs can help students understand their host families better so they can make a smoother adjustment. Sometimes a small change in your behavior can make a major difference in your experience. However, it takes time, and it is not an easy process.

Successful adjustment to another culture requires you to be able to ask for and receive help when you have problems. It is not foolish or immature to ask others to help you through a difficult time. As an exchange student, you may not have enough information to make the best decision. Working through the problems you are having with a concerned, knowledgeable adult from the exchange organization can often aid you in making a successful adjustment. This support is provided by responsible exchange programs for all students. It is not, and never should be allowed to be, a judgment about your own or your host family's worth nor a punishment for mistakes you or they may have made.

If your situation does not improve enough to allow you to live comfortably with your host family, a family change is usually a good solution for all concerned. Though you and your former hosts may have hurt feelings, you will also have some sense of relief. The efforts both you and your family were making in trying to adjust to each other were probably more of a burden than either you or they realized.

Most students who have been dealing with a difficult situation for some time feel much freer and glad for another chance. It is also frightening, though, since no person wants to be faced with another, similar situation in the new family. Fortunately, most students learn a great deal from their first experience and handle the situation differently the second time around. Students who get help with their troubles early in the year have a better chance of successfully completing the year, either with their first hosts or with a second host family. Students who let the problems continue unresolved for months become drained of all their strength, so by the time they do seek help from the exchange organization, an early return home is the only option. So seek assistance soon if you feel the problems with your host family may be irreconcilable even after you have made sincere efforts to solve them.

2. Shorter Exchange Programs

The assumption made in this book is that the exchange student's program lasts for one school year. Not every student stays this long in another country, however. Many opportunities exist for students to try out shorter programs, usually over the summer months or when their own school is not in session.

Usually, the shorter programs are less challenging than the year program. This makes them a good choice for students who are unsure about being away from home for an entire school year. Students on a shorter program will also go through stages of adjustment such as those described in this book. Though their stay may not coincide with any major holidays and they may not have the sense of cabin fever after a long winter indoors, they are likely to go though arrival fatigue, settling in, culture shock, and culture learning. They may not attend school, but they need to adjust to the family and make friends in the community, and the situations they face are very much like those of students in a year-long program. Short-term exchange students who live with host families learn a great deal over the course of six to twelve weeks. For instance, those who have studied the host-country language beforehand may achieve near fluency. Even those who arrive with no knowledge of the language are likely to learn enough for general conversation. Students can expect a significant improvement in their understanding of their host country's culture, though not as great as those who stay for a full year. In other areas of learning, students on shorter programs can be expected to become more adaptable to new environments and to have a greater international awareness and understanding of other cultures.[1]

On the other hand, many students in a summer program barely begin to feel comfortable in the host country before it is time to return home. They do not learn the language as well as those who stay a year, nor do they gain as much understanding of the host country and culture. The personal growth and new insight that mark the year-long program experience may not be fully achieved over the short-term exchange, though in many cases the shorter program provides a good foundation for future learning and is a way to prepare for a longer experience at a later date.

It is also difficult for short-term students to become much more than houseguests in their host familys' homes or develop friendships of any depth outside of the host family. Still, many former exchange students and their summer host families remain in touch for years and visit each other whenever possible.

---

[1] This information emerged from the AFS impact study, in which students on short-term programs showed similar levels of growth to year-program students in several areas and even greater increases in these three areas.

Appendix

What You Should Expect from an Exchange Program

The number of exchange programs for secondary school students has grown dramatically in the past twenty years. In the United States, the Council on Standards for International Educational Travel (CSIET) has developed specific guidelines for exchange programs listed in its annual publication. If you are from the United States or planning to go to the U.S., you should check to see if your program is listed in CSIET's *Advisory List of International Educational Travel and Exchange Programs* (see suggested reading list).

Some exchange programs offer a number of special activities and orientation programs for students, while others simply offer a homestay arrangement. Even in the most basic exchange program, however, the student should expect certain services to be offered.

1. You Should Receive Information before You Depart.

Every exchange organization should provide students with certain basic information before departure. All students should have the name, address, and telephone number of their host families at least one week before they depart from their home countries. Most organizations provide much more information. Frequently, exchange students are able to write to their host families before they leave home, which means receiving the name and address at least three weeks before departure.

Occasionally, students will have temporary arrangements upon their arrival until a permanent host family can be found. Such an arrangement can succeed, but it provides a difficult beginning to the year. Exchange students who have only a temporary arrangement should question the organization further about how a permanent family will be found.

2. You Should Be Met upon Arrival.

Except in very unusual circumstances, every exchange student should be met upon arrival by either the host family or by a representative of the exchange organization, or both. Before arriving in the host community, you may have to change planes once in the host country or switch from the airport to a train or bus. In any case, you should be met at the airport, train station, or bus terminal at your final destination.

There can be delays, of course, because traveling sometimes means connections missed or other unexpected delays. You should not be overly anxious if your host family is not there as soon as you arrive. Your flight might be early. They might have made a mistake about the time. They may be stuck in traffic. They may be in another part of the airport looking for you. For these reasons, and others, you should have a telephone number.

3. You Should Be Given a Telephone Number for Emergencies.

The exchange program should provide you with a way of contacting your hosts if something goes wrong. Most emergencies are not very serious, but when everything is strange and new that is little consolation. You should also have a contact and/or a phone number for someone other than your host family, preferably a representative of the exchange organization.

4. You Should Have Your Own Bed and a Study Area.

While brothers or sisters might share a bed in many countries, an exchange student should not have to do so, even with a host sibling of the same sex and age. The bed you are assigned, however, might not be the kind you are used to. Depending on the host culture, your bed might be a futon that you roll up each morning and put away or a bed that folds into a sofa by day. Your host family will try to do their best to make you comfortable whether they live in a large house or a tiny apartment, but you must be ready to adapt.

If you are going to be attending school, you should also be given a desk or table that you can use for studying. Again, in small homes where space is scarce, your study area might also be the kitchen table or one you share with a host brother or sister.

5. **Your School Arrangements Should Be Made by the Exchange Program.**
If you will be attending school, the exchange program should have made all the necessary arrangements for your admission. Exchange students should not have to find their own schools to attend. On the other hand, if school is not part of the program, you should know this before you leave home.

Suggested Reading List

About Youth Exchange Programs

Council on Standards for International Educational Travel (CSIET). *Advisory List of International Educational Travel and Exchange Programs.* Alexandria, VA: CSIET. Published annually. To obtain copy, write CSIET, 212 South Henry Street, Alexandria, VA 22314.

Grove, Cornelius. *Orientation Handbook for Youth Exchange Programs.* Yarmouth, ME: Intercultural Press, 1989. (out of print)

King, Nancy, and Ken Huff. *Host Family Survival Kit: A Guide for American Host Families,* 2d ed. Yarmouth, ME: Intercultural Press, forthcoming.

Language and Culture Learning (for English speakers)

Experiment in International Living (EIL). *Getting the Whole Picture: A Student's Field Guide to Language Acquisition and Cultural Exploration.* Brattleboro, VT: EIL, 1984. For information write World Learning (formerly Experiment in International Living), Kipling Road, Brattleboro, VT 05301.

Rubin, Joan, and Irene Thompson. *How to be a More Successful Language Learner.* Boston: Heinle & Heinle, 1982.

Understanding the U.S.A. and Other Cultures

Althen, Gary. *American Ways: A Guide for Foreigners in the United States.* Yarmouth, ME: Intercultural Press, 1988.

Carroll, Raymonde. *Cultural Misunderstandings: The French-American Experience.* Chicago: University of Chicago Press, 1988.

Church, Nancy, and Anne Moss. *How to Survive in the U.S.A.: English for Travelers and Newcomers.* Cambridge, UK: Cambridge University Press, 1983.

Gorden, Raymond L. *Living in Latin America: A Case Study in Cross-Cultural Communication.* Skokie, IL: National Textbook, 1974.

Hall, Edward. *The Silent Language*. Garden City, NY: Doubleday, 1959.

Kearny, Edward N., Mary Ann Kearny, and JoAnn Crandall. *The American Way: An Introduction to American Culture*. Englewood Cliffs, NJ: Prentice-Hall, 1984.

Kohls, L. Robert, *Survival Kit for Overseas Living*. Yarmouth, ME: Intercultural Press, 1984.

Miller, Stuart. *Understanding Europeans*. Santa Fe, NM: John Muir Publications, 1987.

Mitchell, Arnold. *The Nine American Lifestyles: Who We Are, Where We Are Going*. New York: Macmillan, 1983.

Smith, Elise, and Louis Fiber Luce, eds. *Toward Internationalism*. Rowley, MA: Newbury House, 1979.

Index

A

accent, speaking with an, 69
adaptation. *See* adjustment
adjustment, 10, 13, 31-43, 82.
    See also culture shock,
    readjustment
adjustment, host family, 10, 45-
    58, 70
adjustment to school, 70-71
advice, sources of, 13-14
Advisory List of International
    Educational Travel and
    Exchange Programs, 119
Althen, Gary, 27
anger, 40, 99
Argentina, 98
arrival fatigue, 32-33. *See also*
    exhaustion, jet lag
Art of Crossing Cultures, The, 26
attributions, 28-30
Australia, 47, 69
Austria, 12, 105

B

babysitter, 3
bedroom, use of, 21, 74
Bennett, Janet and Milton, 27
boarder, exchange student as, 2
Bolivia, 81
boredom, 100
Brazil, 11, 112
Britain, 107

C

Carnival, 90, 92

cars as conversation topic, 18-19
cats, attitude toward, 16-17
changing host families, 115-116
Chile, 12
China, xvi-xvii, 19, 35
Christmas, 90-92
cleanliness. *See* health
clothes, wearing the same, 17-18
clubs, school, 78
Colombia, xvii, 14, 21
community, role in, 6-8
conversation topics, 18-19, 94
counseling, 87
criticism of your country, 7
cross-cultural adaptation. *See*
    adjustment
CSIET, 119
cultural advisors, 45. *See also*
    advice, sources of
cultural assumptions and values,
    15, 24
cultural baggage, 14-16, 18, 21-
    22, 61
cultural differences, 10, 23-30, 59
cultural fatigue, 82. *See also*
    cultural shock
culture, 23-30. *See also* deep
    culture
culture learning, xvii-xviii, 42-
    43, 93-100, 114. *See also*
    culture, studying your own
culture sharing, 76. *See also*
    lifestyle sharing
culture shock, 35-41, 81-87. *See*
    also adjustment, reentry
    shock, reverse culture shock
culture, studying your own, 56
customs, government, 58

125